Living the
Wonder of It All

Living the Wonder of It All

by

Ralph S. Marston, Jr.

IMAGE EXPRESS INC.

Austin, Texas

Living the Wonder of It All
By Ralph S. Marston, Jr.

Distributed by:
    Image Express, Inc.
    P.O. Box 66536
    Austin, TX 78766 USA
    Phone 512-401-4900
    Web: www.greatday.com/books

The Daily Motivator® is a Registered Trademark of
    Ralph S. Marston, Jr.

To read The Daily Motivator on the Internet, visit
    www.DailyMotivator.com

ISBN 0-9664634-1-2
Printed in the United States of America

To my parents, Ralph and Meredith Marston, who continue to inspire, to offer their loving enouragement and support, and who live each moment to the highest standards;

To my wife, Karen, who loves unconditionally no matter what;

And to my daughters, Angela and Kimbie, who humble me daily with their passion for living.

Visit *The Daily Motivator* website at

www.DailyMotivator.com

On *The Daily Motivator* website, you'll find:

- A new, original positive message from Ralph Marston every Monday through Saturday

- Beautiful, calming picture and music presentations including *The Wonder of It All, Right Now* and *Even Now*

- An archive of more than 2,500 previous daily messages

- Online ordering of e-mail subscriptions, gift subscriptions, books and music from *The Daily Motivator*

Access to all of the above is available to everyone who visits, with no subscription required. If you do choose to purchase an e-mail subscription, there's even more, including a new picture and music presentation with each daily message, downloadable e-books, and more.

Also be sure to visit

www.PeaceBeyondWords.com

where you can listen to sample clips from the music CD, *Peace Beyond Words*. The CD includes 15 original instrumental pieces composed by Paul Baker especially for *The Daily Motivator*.

Contents

The Wonder of It All

Do you ever wonder
At the wonder of it all?

Do you ever stand in awe
of the tiniest things
and how perfectly they work together?

Do you ever stop to think
about all the possibilities
and how even though they have no limit
they grow in number with every minute?

Do you ever wonder
when the leaves flutter down in autumn
at the incomprehensible power of life
that brings them back in spring?

Do you watch the waves roll in
and then look out far beyond them
where the water seems to touch the sky
and realize
that the vast expanse before your eyes
is only a small little corner
of all there really is?

And do you comprehend that all there really is,
as unimaginably grand as it may seem,
is only a smaller corner still
of all that there can be?

Do you ever wonder
how love can stay alive
past every pleasure and every pain
and even when there can be no hope
there is more than ever?

Do you ever struggle to lift a heavy rock and wonder
how a massive mountain can rise
thousands of feet above the plain
without even trying?

Do you ever realize that
no matter how much you may know,
no matter how many wonders you may have experienced,
there will always, always be more?

Do you ever wonder
why it is you wonder
and why you know what beauty is
even though you can't define it?

Do you ever wonder
who is doing the wondering,
who is looking out through your eyes
and feeling completely at home
with the wonder of it all?

Whatever you believe,
whatever you profess,
whatever you doubt or fear or hope for,
there are some things
your heart cannot deny
when you let go
and let yourself know
the wonder of it all.

Introduction

The title of this book came to me as I walked in the woods behind my house on a cool, bright morning in early autumn. A golden leaf fluttered to the ground, then another one followed, and another and another. As I stood there surrounded by the brilliant spectacle, I realized I was witnessing something that had been happening, right there in that spot, for perhaps thousands and thousands of years. At that moment, I felt thoroughly blessed to be living the wonder of it all.

As I watched each leaf fall to the ground, I thought of the almost unimaginable forces working in perfect harmony to cause such a seemingly simple event. The tilt of our massive planet on its axis and its journey around the sun, the process of photosynthesis in the cells of the trees, the ever-present influence of gravity, the oceanic and atmospheric factors creating a breeze in the air, and many, many more things than can possibly be imagined were all coming together to send a tiny leaf on its brief journey from a branch of the tree to the ground.

We are always immersed in the wonder of it all, yet too often we fail to even begin to appreciate it. We see the leaves falling and then reappearing in the spring, perhaps we admire their beauty, and yet we move hurriedly on without fully appreciating, without fully living the wonder of what we're experiencing. We hurry and worry, struggle and strive, and in the process we often overlook many of the most useful and valuable qualities of living. We need continual reminders to re-focus our thoughts on the things that really matter, and that's what *The Daily Motivator* is all about.

For more than eight years, I've been writing brief, positive reminders of those values and those qualities that enable us to truly live the wonder of it all. Each Monday through Saturday since November 1995, *The Daily Motivator* website has offered a new, original message designed to help readers remember, appreciate and experience how beautiful and full of wonder life can be. In this book you'll find some of the best of those messages.

Since 1995, I've written more than 2,500 daily messages. And while each one is unique (they never repeat), there are several themes that are continually reinforced as the years go by. Those themes correspond to the fundamental values and qualities necessary for successfully living the wonder of it all. Each chapter in this book addresses one of those qualities, and includes several messages which explore the subject from many different angles.

I hope you'll view this book not as a step-by-step how-to manual, but rather as a collection of reminders that will help you to appreciate and to fully live the wonder of it all.

Ralph Marston
November 2003

Living the Wonder of It All

Living With Gratitude

Lead with gratitude

Make gratitude your first response and it will soon become an empowering perspective from which you can achieve great things. Rather than looking for something to criticize, look for things to genuinely praise. Make the most positive qualities the first things you notice in people, in your surroundings, and in the situations which come along.

There are positive sides and negative sides to everything. The negative aspects will have little trouble asserting themselves. They need no help from you. Don't overlook them, but don't give your energy to them either.

Put your focus on finding a reason for gratitude. It's there, no matter what. From that you can build and grow, move ahead and prosper. Make it a habit on a moment by moment basis. Ingrain it in your very being. Let it become second nature to you to seek the positive and you will indeed find it. It's an approach which will bring delightful substance to your relationships and powerful effectiveness to your pursuits.

Lead with gratitude and you'll truly be even more grateful for the richness of living which most certainly will follow.

Something to appreciate

A great way to remain positively focused is to have something positive toward which you can direct your thoughts at a moment's notice. That way, when you catch yourself falling into negative thought patterns you can quickly switch your thoughts somewhere else.

Imagine what would happen if you made a habit, at the beginning of each day, of finding something new to appreciate about yourself, your life, or your world. Then, any time you felt yourself being drawn into negative, destructive thinking, you could immediately put your focus on that day's object of appreciation and gratitude.

Genuine, heartfelt gratitude can have a powerful positive influence on every aspect of your life. It can be an effective counterbalance to all the negativity the world throws your way.

Think right now of something for which you can be truly grateful. Then, the next time you feel yourself being drawn into anger, frustration, spite, envy or despair, shift your focus instead to your ready-made gratitude.

Keep yourself genuinely and realistically positive with sincere gratitude. And each day will bring even more reasons to be thankful.

Honor

Honor this beautiful day by making the most of it. Honor your skills and abilities by making full use of them. Honor the people around you by acting respectfully and responsibly.

No matter what kind of troubles you may have, just think of how fortunate you are to be alive and living in a world where almost anything is possible. Consider for a moment the good things you have, and the good things that you can accomplish through your willingness, determination and action.

Honor and appreciate the good things you have by seeing the positive in every situation. Honor your work by giving it value and making it count. Honor the powerful bundle of possibilities that is your life. Make the most of every single moment. The things you honor will grow, bringing many blessings to enrich your world.

Build on your blessings

Right this moment, there are many, many things for which you can be thankful. Have you stopped lately to think of them all? Life may often seem difficult, and indeed it is in many ways. Yet for all life's difficulties, still you have a multitude of blessings, most of which are too often taken for granted.

Think of five things, right now, for which you can be thankful today. Think of five blessings, and you'll uncover five valuable treasures which can help you to grow, to build, to create, to move your life forward.

Don't be so busy seeking treasure outside yourself, that you fail to make the most of the treasures you already have. Rather, nurture and appreciate the blessings you have, and they will grow into more abundant blessings.

Success is not something you come upon all of a sudden. It is something which grows outward from inside of you. It is a blessing you already have, which you nurture until it blossoms. Appreciate what you have, as often and as fully as you can. Nurture your blessings, with your focus and your effort, and they'll grow into all you could ever desire.

A privilege

When you're tempted to give in to anger, resentment, self-pity, envy, or other feelings of negativity, remember this: life is a privilege, not a punishment.

Think of how a tiny insect acts to save its own life when injured or threatened. Consider the compelling wisdom in that instinct for self preservation. Life is precious to the living, no matter how seemingly insignificant. It is a privilege worth preserving and nurturing.

Life is a privilege, not a punishment. Think about that. Look at your attitude, consider your actions, from the perspective that life is indeed a privilege. Why would you ever want to complain about anything?

You're not a victim. You're a miracle. You have precious life, and it is magnificent. Keep that in mind, and live it accordingly.

Envy

Whatever you value and appreciate, will grow. True abundance begins with gratitude, because gratitude focuses energy on the positive side of life.

Envy works in direct opposition to gratitude. It fosters an attitude of lack and limitation. It promotes anger and resentment. Envy focuses your energy on your lack of abundance. As a result, you see the problems and not the opportunities. You look for reasons why things will not work, instead of looking for ways to make them work. You look for excuses, instead of looking for solutions.

Envy is rooted in a zero-sum mentality which assumes that one person's good fortune comes at the expense of others. That may have been a valid assumption five hundred years ago. It is most certainly not the case now.

Why would you ever want to be envious, when all it does is

bring you down? Rejoice in the good fortune of others. Use it is a source of inspiration, and as a reason for expressing gratitude. By so doing, you increase the abundance in your own life.

Having enough

In the frantic rush to get more, we often deny ourselves the richness of having enough. Think for a moment how satisfying it would be to have enough of the things you need — enough money, a big enough home, enough time, enough friends, enough interesting things to do. Yet if you're always striving to get more, then you can never have enough.

Having enough is just as much a result of your attitude as it is a function of your bank account. When you have enough, you can truly enjoy it. Having enough of anything does not in any way prevent you from getting more. In fact, having enough very often leads to having more.

Abundance flows steadily and reliably from gratitude. Yet it is difficult to express gratitude when you're continually focused on getting more. How can you be fully appreciative of what you have when you don't consider it to be enough? How can you experience abundance when your mind is filled with thoughts of lack and limitation?

Is ambition stifled by having enough? No, because along with the sincere gratitude of having enough comes the eagerness to make the most of it. Continually focus on making the best of what you have, and you will always have enough.

Thankfully resourceful

When suddenly faced with a challenging situation, we tend to focus on the oppressive negative aspects of that situation. Consequently we can quickly become overwhelmed.

A more positive approach is to identify the aspects of the situation for which you can be thankful. It may sound a little absurd, when confronted with a difficult challenge, to look for ways to be grateful for it. And yet that is an excellent place to begin.

There's a word for people who take this approach. We call them resourceful. That moniker comes not because these people have access to any more resources than anyone else, but rather because they are able to clearly identify and make use of those resources, particularly in the midst of difficulty.

Resourcefulness grows from an attitude of gratitude. Rather than bemoaning your fate, shine a thankful light on your situation and you'll illuminate much value. Ask yourself, "What can I be thankful for here?" The things you find will likely make the difference between winning and losing.

The little things

Often it is difficult to truly experience gratitude for the big, important things. Yes, we can say we're thankful and certainly on an intellectual level we are. Yet somehow the monumental blessings are difficult to fully grasp.

The little things, though, are much closer and therefore more intense. It is toward those little things that we can most easily experience a warm and palpable, encompassing gratitude. It is in thankfulness for the little things that we can know the sweet and sustaining flavor of true appreciation.

And in so doing, we realize that the little things are not so little after all. For the big, momentous things in life are nothing more than a lot of little things strung carefully together.

Be thankful for the little things, for that warm ray of sunshine beaming through your window, for the refreshing cool wind against your face, for the joy of helping a child to experience something new, for the savory aroma of freshly baked bread. In your retail thankfulness, the depth of your wholesale gratitude for all that is life will grow strong indeed.

Ever thankful

When some things go wrong, take a moment to be thankful for the many more things that are still going right. To find a sure and dependable way through your troubles, start by counting your blessings.

Focus on what you can do and you won't have to be held back by what you cannot do. Value and appreciate what you do have, and you will no longer be limited by what you don't have.

True abundance begins with gratitude. The more thankful you are for the good things you have, the more they will grow to have even greater value.

With gratitude in your heart, your eyes can see more clearly. You'll discover ways for moving forward that you otherwise would never have noticed.

Before you blame, before you worry, before you resent or despair, take a moment to be truly thankful. See the world from the perspective of gratitude and see what a powerful positive difference it can make.

Let your blessings compel you

Stop for a moment and consider all the good things which you too often take for granted — your health, your family, the air you breathe, the water you drink, your home, your community, the magnificent universe around you, your faith, your friends, the knowledge you possess, your skills, and so much more.

Indeed, you are blessed. You are filled with possibilities. Yet what good are your blessings if you're not making the most of them? Of what value are your possibilities if you do not make the effort to fulfill them?

Think of the good things you have going for you. There may be many or there may be few. What matters most, is that you get them to grow. That comes from gratitude and appreciation.

When you truly appreciate your blessings, they become powerfully compelling. And they grow, filling your life with quality and excellence, and compelling you to reach even higher.

Gratitude and thankfulness are more than just words or thoughts. To truly appreciate the good things in your life, you must take the actions necessary to nurture and defend them.

You're blessed with a great starting point. Let your many blessings compel you to reach ever higher.

Living With Authenticity

Be you

The surest way to make a good impression is to be yourself. After all, being you is what you do best. You have a great deal of experience at it. The surest way to look like a fool is by attempting to impress others with something you're not.

Success comes not from pretense. Success comes from substance. Perhaps you think the substance of your life is not that impressive. If so, you're completely and absolutely wrong!

You are overflowing with substance and value and it will show if you'll just let it. Your own experiences, thoughts, interests, knowledge, passions, desires, integrity and sense of humor, among many other things, set you apart and make you truly special.

You are wonderful and you are worthy. The power of substance comes from being who you are. Be you. It is your destiny. The world is waiting to joyfully throw its arms around the genuine, valuable person you know you are.

The freedom of truth

The truth of who you are is much more beautiful and valuable than any deception you could construct. The more honest you are with yourself and with others, the more you'll tap into the real and lasting value in your life.

When you tell a lie or hide the truth, it brings you down. When you deceive or exaggerate to make yourself look better, you're sending a negative, destructive message to yourself. Consider the damage to your own confidence that occurs when you attempt to appear as someone you're not, just to win the approval of others. The person you pretend to be can never even come close to being as valuable as the person you really are.

Live in truth and let the real person you are shine brightly. Respect and value what is true, rather than what is convenient for the moment. When seeking to be the best you can be, nothing is more important than living truthfully. Be who you are, tell it like it is, and enjoy the real and lasting freedom of the truth.

The real thing

Arrogance is a poor substitute for confidence. Taking is a poor substitute for creating. Possessing is a poor substitute for appreciating.

Staying busy is a poor substitute for accomplishing something. Anger is a poor substitute for discipline. Rudeness is a poor substitute for eloquence. Aloofness is a poor substitute for joy. Envy is a poor substitute for effort.

Rationalization is a poor substitute for truth. Artful deceit is a poor substitute for integrity. Promises are a poor substitute for commitment. Gluttony is a poor substitute for nourishment. Stylishness is a poor substitute for courtesy.

Why settle for a meager substitute when you can have the real thing? Why bother with outward appearances when you can enjoy the genuine substance of life? Get real. Make the effort to be true to your best values. Live the real thing. It's worth it.

The side of the truth

Truth is one of the most effective tools available to you. When you respect, honor and abide in the truth, you put yourself on the side of strength and power.

You can try to cover it up, explain it away, run from it or rationalize against it, but in the end if you go against the truth you will lose. Lies, deceit, half truths, rationalizations and justifications must constantly be defended and maintained, and will eventually crumble. The truth remains the truth whether it is defended or not.

It often can seem convenient or expedient to deny the truth. But when you deny the truth you put yourself in a position of weakness. Making a habit of that can drain your energy, not to mention your credibility.

Put yourself on the side of the truth, though it may be inconvenient or even painful. There will surely come a time when you'll be glad you did.

Credibility

Nothing which could ever be gained by deceit is worth the cost. Once credibility has been lost, it might never be completely regained. Without credibility, it is impossible to sustain any kind of success. In an environment of distrust and suspicion, very little can ever get done.

Promises and commitments are not just devices for achieving the purpose of the moment. In the bigger picture, they have the very real potential to either build credibility, or to consume it. As such, commitments must be carefully chosen and promises prudently made with consideration for whether or not they can be followed through.

A reputation, once tarnished, is exceedingly difficult to rebuild. Better to put your efforts into keeping that reputation strong, positive and growing rather than working to defend it from your own folly.

A strong and genuine degree of credibility can take you a long way. Be careful not to compromise this valuable asset for the convenience of the moment. Stay true to your word, honor your commitments, and reap the immense long-term value which can be achieved in no other way.

What you know is right

No matter what you do, there will be people who disapprove of it. You cannot please everyone, so it is foolish to even try. Instead, guide your actions by what you know is true. Go beyond what is merely popular, or expected, or what looks impressive. Keep your focus on what is right.

Graciously and humbly accept praise without living for it. Learn from criticism without being dismayed by it. Listen to your heart. Live life on your own terms, based on what you know is the right thing to do. Those who are worth impressing will be most impressed by authenticity.

You have many special things to offer the world. Some people will resent you. Others will blindly accept you. Don't let yourself be swayed by either. Be who you are, as honestly as you can.

Integrity is more than just a claim or a promise. Integrity results from being consistently true to your most profound val-

Living the Wonder of It All

ues, even when no one is looking. Fulfill your enormous positive possibilities by continuing to do what you know is right.

Simple or easy?

There's a big difference between simple answers and easy answers. Simple answers are usually powerful and effective, yet challenging. Easy answers are usually appealing, but not very effective, and can even be dangerous.

Let's say you need to lose weight. The simple answer is — get more regular exercise and eat a more nutritionally balanced diet. That's simple enough, and though often difficult to follow, usually effective. The easy answer is — take this pill and eat anything you want. Very appealing, but it probably won't work.

You can spot an easy answer because it is something you want to hear. Even though it may not make much sense, if you want to hear it badly enough you can make yourself believe it. You can spot simple answers because they seem so obvious, even though they may be a bit challenging.

When there's a simple answer and an easy answer, the best choice is almost always the simple answer. It may not be what you want to hear, but it is probably what you need to do.

Live in truth

More things can be accomplished more quickly in a situation where there is trust among everyone involved. Trust can often make the difference between success and failure.

Trust grows and thrives when there is a genuine commitment to truth. Truth is not always convenient or easy. It is often difficult and awkward. Yet truth is an absolute necessity for building trust, and without trust it is difficult to get anything accomplished.

Even liars demonstrate a respect for the truth, though sadly they also demonstrate an ignorance of how to attain it. A lie would have no purpose if there was no truth. Yet the real, lasting power of truth comes only from being truthful.

There are countless ways to evade the truth. They are all, in the end, a tragic waste of effort. Truth is just as essential to nourish the mind as is food to nourish the body. The more fully you live each moment in truth, the more powerful and effective those moments will be.

From the heart

The way to appear sincere is to actually be sincere. The way to gain the trust of others is to live with uncompromising integrity. The way to be believed, and to be believable, is to always speak the truth. The way to show how much you care, is to really, truly care.

The way to speak to the heart of another is to speak from your own heart. Clever words and fancy trappings will soon fade, and the real substance of the person behind them is what will be remembered.

The most effective strategy for successful living is really no strategy at all. It is, rather, to be real, to be honest, to be authentic, to be you.

There's no value in pretending to be someone you are not. When you speak from the heart and act from the heart, who you really are is always more than enough.

Living With a Positive Attitude

Good news

Today, millions of people will drive to work and back again in comfort and safety without having an accident. Today, people will fall in love and that love will last a lifetime. Today, millions of people will volunteer their time and donate their money to others who are in need. Today, countless numbers of people all over the world will live through a peaceful, productive day.

Today, exciting new discoveries will be made. New homes will be built. Imaginations will be sparked. Lives will be saved. Friendships will be renewed. Children will be cared for.

Between now and the time tomorrow begins, a million million good, worthy things will have taken place. Today is full of positive opportunity, and much of it will be realized.

Is there turmoil and strife in the world? Yes, of course there is. Yet there is much good as well. And it is so commonplace, so pervasive, so much an accepted and expected part of life that it doesn't even make the news.

When you hear about the negative, remember this. There's a lot more positive. So much that we take it for granted. On the whole, today is so great and wonderful as to be beyond comprehension.

The success response

Banks are more likely to lend money to people who have proven in the past that they can make money. Employers are more likely to hire employees who have proven in the past that they can get things done.

People who have been successful in the past, are likely to be successful in the future. Why? Is it just that they're luckier? Do they have some kind of inside secret? Do they somehow manage to avoid the challenges and attract the best opportunities? No.

Successful people live in the same world as everyone else, with the same challenges, the same knowledge, the same amount of luck. The difference between success and mediocrity is not in what we're confronted with, but in how we respond to it.

The successful response is to find the positive aspect of any situation, and then to apply that positive force toward accomplishing the goal at hand. No matter what the circumstance, some degree of success is attainable. Seeing it and consistently reaching for it is what sets the winners in life apart from the rest. Anyone can do it. It's all in how you respond.

Life's hopes

Darkness has no place to hide when the midday sun shines, brightly persistent. Fill your life, your thoughts, your actions with goodness, and there will be scant room for despair.

Though turmoil may be all around, you set your own standards, you define the quality of your own thoughts, you control your own conduct. You can rise above the rest, not because you are inherently better, but because of the choices you make.

Living the Wonder of It All

Your good fortune comes not from fads, trends, or clever deception, for those things never last. It comes from your own commitment to excellence, from the value you create, from the true and meaningful difference you make.

Rise above the shoving fray, not out of spite but compelled by the irrefutable possibilities which this life presents. You are meant for excellence. Live up to life's hopes for you.

Thought power

What would you fear if you knew for certain that your fear would bring it upon you? On what dream would you focus the power of attention and commitment if you knew, without a doubt, that your commitment would make it real?

At any given time, there is a thought living in your mind. Everything you've ever accomplished, came to you through a series of thoughts. Every fear that has ever held you back, came to you as a thought.

There is awesome power in a tiny drop of rain, when with other drops it gathers into a mighty storm. Similarly, each thought is a small thing, lasting only a moment and then gone, only to be replaced by another. Yet when many thoughts are all focused in the same direction, there is no limit to their power.

Your thoughts will come and they will go. They are yours to use. Gather enough thoughts together in the service of a common goal, and you will make it happen.

Do what can't be done

Do they say it can't be done? Then find a way to do it. Anything that is considered impossible is an opportunity waiting to be harvested. Just imagine the incredible power of being able to say "I can" when everyone else is saying "I can't."

"I can't" usually means "I won't." Be the person who will, and a world of opportunity opens up to you. It is easy to say "no," to avoid the challenge and the effort. Success comes to those who say "yes," and then set about to make it happen.

Complaints and excuses will keep you imprisoned in a tedious world of mediocrity. Yet what is impossible for others, does not have to be for you. Welcome the challenges. Take the initiative. Feel the satisfaction of accomplishing that which has never before been attempted.

Look for things which can't or won't be done. Be the one who makes them happen, and reap their enormous value.

One thing

Try this. Every time you encounter someone new, make it a point to find at least one thing positive about them. Each time you hear a news item, find at least one thing positive about it. When some new situation comes up — at work, at home, in your community, with your family — look for at least one positive aspect.

Living positively means actively seeking out the positive elements in everything you encounter. Sure, it's easy to be upbeat when everything is going your way. Anyone can do that. It is far more important, however, to take a positive approach in circumstances that most people would view as negative.

Winners are not positive because they're lucky. Winners have good luck because they are focused on the positive. There is a positive way to respond, even in the most dire situations. Look for the good. Look for the positive. It is always there.

Enthusiasm

Enthusiasm can win over even the most ardent skeptic. When you truly believe in what you are doing, it shows. And it pays. The winners in life are those who are excited about where they're going.

Be genuinely enthusiastic, and you'll be impossible to ignore. Show enthusiasm, and it will spread. People are drawn to enthusiasm.

Find a way to be truly enthusiastic about what you're doing. If you can't muster any enthusiasm, then why in the world are you doing it? There are so many opportunities in this life. Do you really want to waste your precious time in the service of something which does not even warrant your own enthusiasm?

Be as effective as you can be by infusing your actions with enthusiasm. Nothing is more insincere than phony enthusiasm. Don't fake it. Be truly enthusiastic. Get excited, and let it show.

Unaffordable extravagance

Negative thinking is perhaps the most extravagant, wasteful indulgence imaginable. It is something which no one alive can truly afford.

The price which negative thinking extracts can never be regained, because the price of negative thinking is paid with life. How is it possible for anyone to replace a moment, or a day or a year lost to negativity? And beyond the lost opportunity that it represents, negative thinking is just plain destructive. It accomplishes nothing and it costs so much.

Fortunately, negative thinking is completely unnecessary. And it is completely under your control. You don't have to participate in it if you don't want to. And why in the world would you ever want to?

No matter what comes your way, you can decide how to respond. Even in the most seemingly hopeless of situations, the best course is to remain focused on the positive, on what you can do, on the difference you can make. Why would you possibly want to do anything else?

Stop digging

It is true that you must pay the price for your past mistakes. Yet that does not mean that you must keep making them. So often we adopt an attitude of "I'll never get out of this" and it becomes a self-fulfilling prophecy. The truth is, you can start to get out of it right now, no matter what has happened in the past. You cannot change the past or its consequences, but you can immediately change the present, and make the future look infinitely brighter.

When you find yourself in a hole, it often seems that the only thing to do is to keep digging. But that will only get you in deeper. The first thing you must do is stop digging. As soon as you stop digging, even before you start climbing out, you've made a positive change.

Momentum can work either for you or against you, and it all depends on what direction you're going. Momentum is not dependent on where you are, just on which way you're headed.

You can have positive momentum right this moment, regardless of what has happened in the past. All it takes is a change in direction. All it takes is to stop digging, and start climbing out. You got yourself here, and you can get yourself wherever you want to go. Direct your momentum toward where you want to be, and don't stop until you're there.

Upside potential

Life is biased toward the positive. You can only fall so far, but there is no limit to how high you can soar. There are points at which life cannot get any worse, but there is no point at which things cannot get better. You can only lose so much, but there is no limit to what you can gain.

With every setback comes a real opportunity to grow and move forward. And with every triumph, further triumphs become more likely. In every situation there is positive potential.

Yes, the risks are there. Yet the risks are finite. Possibilities are infinite. Consider the incredible upside potential of your own life. No matter where you are, no matter what circumstances you find yourself in, your possibilities always outweigh your problems. Those positive possibilities are yours for the living.

Get real

You can admit reality without admitting defeat. Accepting things for what they are does not prevent you from changing them. Rather, the opposite is true. As soon as you can clearly see and own up to your weaknesses, you have begun to do something about them.

No one is perfect. Everyone is burdened with their own shortcomings. The difference between success and disappointment is whether the shortcomings are a starting point or an excuse.

Your life has a certain reality right now, and you have the ability to change that reality. To change it, you must first see it for what it is. You cannot get to where you want to go if you're unclear about where you are.

You are what you are. That's not an excuse to give up, it is a challenge to move forward. You are what you are, and you have every ability to be what you want to be.

Smile

Right now, think of something pleasant, something positive and uplifting, and smile. Think of someone special, of how they brighten your life. Recall that gloriously beautiful day last week, and how great you felt. Remember how happy your children were to see you last night. Find something that will make you smile, and smile.

It's almost impossible to be negative when you're sincerely smiling. Smile, and you'll be tuning yourself into the positive possibilities of life. Smile with sincerity, with your eyes and your face as well as your lips, and you'll naturally bring out the best in the people around you.

Smile at the people who pass you on the freeway. Smile as you talk on the phone. Even though the person on the other end cannot see your smile, it will still come across the line and inject a positive energy into the conversation.

Smile as much as you can. Come on... smile! A smile can work wonders. Put it to work for you.

How silly

Someday you'll see how silly it is to think you can profit from the misfortune of others. Someday you'll see how silly it is to expect to get something for nothing.

Someday you'll see how silly it is to spend so much time all puffed up with pride and arrogance. One day you'll realize how silly it is to think that you're superior to anyone else.

You'll also understand one day how silly it is to think that any task is beneath you. And there will come a time when you'll see how silly it is to get all worked up and angry over the smallest, most insignificant things.

Someday you'll see how silly it is to consume yourself with worry about what others think of you. And someday you'll see how silly it is to ignore those things that matter most, just for the sake of a quick, fleeting pleasure.

Someday you'll regret all the silliness. And then you'll move beyond it to a place where you can truly live with meaning and purpose and integrity, and with real joy. Wouldn't it be great to be there now? How silly it is to wait any longer.

Knowing and Understanding Yourself

Who are you? How do you define yourself? What makes you different? What makes you special? What unique contribution do you have to make to this world? How can you fulfill your own magnificent possibilities?

These are questions we rarely have the time or the inclination to ponder. Most of our days are filled with accomplishing certain tasks. If we ever look beyond the day-to-day tasks, we begin to consider our longer term goals. Yet, there is something even beyond the goals. Each of us has a unique life purpose. Though we seldom think about it, it makes itself known in many ways. Those who are true to their purpose find happiness, fulfillment and success. Those who act in opposition to their purpose encounter a great deal of frustration and disillusionment.

You know your e-mail address, you know your telephone number, you know the name of the street where you live, you know your job description. You know how tall you are, how much you weigh, what kinds of foods you like. These are all things that describe you, yet they do not truly define you. Your outward and visible characteristics are, at best, circumstantial evidence of the unique person that is you.

Most of us don't pay a lot of attention to discovering, understanding and nurturing our essential selves. Yet it can be very helpful to put some effort — and it does indeed take effort — into learning more about the person inside. What if you were spending every day working against yourself? How much would you get accomplished? What if, each morning, you worked for several hours preparing proposals for clients, then you went to lunch, and, after lunch you spent the afternoon ripping up the proposals and tossing the torn pages into the trash can. What purpose would that serve?

If you're not acquainted with your own essential self, you could be doing something very similar. You could be working all day, every day, to create things for which you have no use or desire. The better you know and understand yourself, the more effectively you can get things done. When you have a solid understanding of your own unique nature, you're able to harness your immense personal power, rather than having to work against it.

Too often we make choices based on other people's values, or to serve the expediency of the moment. And then we wonder why life seems so empty and frustrating. Someone will enter a profession in which he has little interest or aptitude, because the money is good, and will then wonder why his career seems to be going nowhere.

Sure, money is critically important. However, there are many, many ways to make money. And your best prospect for being financially successful is to work with passion and commitment. That means doing something that interests you, excites you, and challenges you in a positive way — something which is in line with the true person you are inside. It means doing something which demands the best of you, and takes advantage of your own unique strengths, so that you can create the most value for your effort.

Finding yourself is not a matter of rejecting those around you, or of abandoning your responsibilities. It is a matter of relating to those people, and carrying out those responsibilities in a more genuine way, of tapping into the immense power of your own essence. It's not about joining some cult or abandoning your faith. It is about strengthening the connections between your true self and the things that are important to you. It is about understanding yourself and your priorities, and using that understanding to become more effective in everything you do.

When you become better acquainted with who you are, you're better able to see positive possibilities in every situation. You're able to better understand your frustrations, and find realistic ways out of them. You're able to more clearly see the incredible possibilities for your own life, and how you can fulfill those possibilities to live with purpose, joy and true fulfillment.

What are you looking for?

So, you've decided you need to "find yourself." What precisely are you looking for? Mainly you want to take an objective look at the things that make you you. These attributes include your life's purpose, your vast array of skills, your hidden wealth, your passions, your most effective state, your priorities, and the things which motivate you to take action. You're looking primarily for inner characteristics and patterns in your life.

So how do you get in touch with yourself, how do you discover and appreciate the beautiful, unique person who lives inside of all your superficial trappings? How do you discover the passionate, purposeful person who lies at the heart of all you do?

The main thing you have to do is look. That sounds simplistic

Living the Wonder of It All

and obvious, yet so many times people don't even think of themselves beyond the superficial level of appearance, possessions and tasks. There is so much more to you than what you look like, what you have, or even what you do. There is someone inside who has unique values, desires and dreams. The inner you has a very definite mission, and a burning passion for that mission. And when you make the effort to look, you'll start to see it.

An effective way to better understand yourself is through a series of probing, introspective questions. It's best if you answer these questions in writing, so you can go back and review your thoughts with some degree of objectivity. It is important to be honest, thoughtful, and as complete as possible when answering the questions. You're doing this for yourself, to help you understand how to better live in harmony with your own purpose. No one else needs to see your answers, so be as open, honest and forthcoming with yourself as possible.

Questions to stimulate self discovery

There are no right or wrong answers to these questions. They are designed for the sole purpose of helping you to think, and to better understand yourself. So, take some thoughtful time with these questions, and enjoy getting to know the special person you are.

What kinds of things did you enjoy as a child, particularly between the ages of 7 and 14? As a child, you were most likely not burdened with the need to make a living, or to impress other people. You did what you did because you wanted to do it. You were in touch with your deepest desires and you followed them. Think of the hobbies you had, the things you did with your friends, the way you spent your time when you were away from school. What were your favorite toys and why did you like them so much? What did you dream of becoming when you "grew up"? The purpose and passion which drove your behavior as a child is still with you. And now, you're in a far better position to express that passion. So go back and remember your childhood. Make an effort to re-connect with that passion, and let it ignite your life.

Has there ever been a time in your life when you were consumed with passion for something? Perhaps it was a course of study, a construction project, a special relationship, a spiritual awakening, volunteer work, a job, a project, a competitive sport, a scientific investigation, an organization of which you were a member, or a trip somewhere. Think about the experience and how it made you feel. Consider why you were attracted to it. How did you describe or express your passion to other people during this time? How do you talk about it now? What was it inside of you that was so ignited by this passion? What would it take to induce a similar passion today?

Think of the people you enjoy being with. Why do you like to be around them? What is it inside of you that relates to them? What do you admire in them? What kinds of activities do you most enjoy doing with these people? Do you most enjoy being with people who are very much like you, who share a similar set of ideas and lifestyle, or do you prefer being with those who are different than you?

What do people compliment you about or commend you for? Think of the things for which you have received praise. What things have you done that have caused others to look up to you? When other people sincerely seek your advice and expertise, what kinds of things do they ask about? In what areas do those around you regularly ask you for your help?

Think of a time when you were extremely satisfied with yourself, and describe the experience in detail. What did you do to bring on this satisfaction? What inner resources did you call upon during this period of accomplishment? What motivated you to take the necessary action? What kept you going even in the face of disappointment? Why did you set out to accomplish it in the first place? What deeply held values of yours were validated by this satisfying experience? Think of two or three accomplishments that would give you a similar degree of satisfaction if you were to achieve them. What things give you satisfaction on a daily basis? What makes them so appealing to you, and what motivates you to continue doing them?

What people do you admire and why do you admire them? Do they have qualities that you see, or would like to see, in yourself? If so, what are those qualities? Are these people living in a way that you would like to live? If so, describe that lifestyle in detail and explain why it appeals to you. Do you admire these people because of their commitment to certain values? If so, what are those values and how do you regularly express your commitment to the same values?

How would you live your life if you had plenty of time and money, and if all the day-to-day problems and challenges were gone? You probably spend so much of your time and energy just making sure that the bills get paid and the roof doesn't leak, that there's barely time to even think about anything else. But if all that suddenly were taken care of, what would you do? What would give you fulfillment? Imagine for a moment that someone has just handed you 25 million dollars. Suddenly, you no longer need to work for a living. You no longer need to impress anyone. You're free to live exactly as you please. What would you do with your time and money, and why? How would you prevent yourself from becoming bored? How would you fill each day with challenge and purpose? Think about that, and you'll learn a lot about yourself.

Along those same lines, consider this. What things would you do even if you would never be paid for doing them? Get rid of the 25 million dollars now, and imagine that you're struggling financially, working hard each week to pay all the bills. In such a circumstance, are there things you would do even though they could not possibly bring you income? Of course you would take care of your family and your own basic necessities of life. Beyond that, though, is there anything so compelling that you would spend your precious time on it just for the love of it?

If you could easily change your behavior, to make yourself happier, what would you change? What beliefs or circumstances have prevented you from changing that behavior in the past? What things in your life would be different if you did change the behavior? Why are these things important to you?

What things in your life are you the most thankful for? How do you protect and nurture them? Why are they so important to you. How do they give you strength, and help you to live with joy? Is there anything that you would be even more thankful for, if you had it?

If you had to live for a year in complete isolation, cut off from the rest of the world, what five things would you bring with you (other than items for your nourishment, health and safety)? Why would each of these items be so important to you, and what would you do with them? How would you prepare yourself mentally for this period of isolation? What personal goals would you plan to accomplish during this period?

Take out your checkbook or credit card statement and look at the items you have purchased over the last few months. Pay particular attention to the discretionary items — things you didn't absolutely have to have, but you bought because you wanted to. What was it about each of these things that appealed to you? Did you buy them with the expectation of solving a particular problem, or in hopes of enjoying a certain kind of pleasure, or did you make some purchases mainly out of curiosity. Which of the products lived up to, or exceeded, your expectations? Is there anything that you don't really need, that you still would very much like to purchase if you had enough money? Why do you want it? How will it bring enjoyment to you?

When you suddenly find yourself with unexpected free time, how do you usually spend that time? What things do you consider to be a waste of time, and why? Time is something that is limited for everyone. No matter what kind of job you have, or where you live, or how much money you have, there are only 24 hours in each day. Think about how you prioritize your time, and consider what that says about your overall priorities. Time is one of the most precious things you have, and the way you use it is a good indicator of the things that are most important to you.

Finally, ask yourself what's most important to you about each of the different areas of your life, such as your job, your home, family, faith, leisure activities, friends, health, and so on. When you determine what's important, then ask yourself what is important about that. For example, you might ask yourself what is most important to you about your job. The answer might be "making money." So then, ask yourself what is important about making money. The answer might be "so I can support my family." Then, consider what is important to you about supporting your family. Is it out of love, a sense of obligation, or something else. Continue this line of questioning as far as you possibly can. Ask what's important, and then consider what's important about that. You'll soon get very deep into your own profoundly held values, and develop a much clearer understanding of what makes you tick.

We're each so close to our own selves, that we often take much of our uniqueness for granted. We think of ourselves as part of the world we live in, and too often we go no deeper than that.

You are special, and have much to contribute. The more you understand yourself, the more you understand the things that drive you and motivate you, the more you'll be able to accomplish. You are full of countless possibilities, each of them unique to you and you alone. Make the effort to know and understand yourself, and those possibilities will start turning into reality.

Living With Acceptance

Acceptance

To change anything for the better, you must first accept it as it is. Acceptance is not the same as approval. Acceptance is not the same as giving up. In fact, acceptance puts us in a better position to carry on.

There is no point in fighting against the way things are. Far better to work toward things as you wish them to be. Denial gets you nowhere. Action gets you anywhere, when it has a clearly defined focus.

Accept what is, understand it and let it be. It is your starting point. To achieve anything, you must clearly and precisely define what you wish to accomplish. Then, you must determine exactly how you will get there. And for that, you must first accept where you are.

It is of little value to find your destination on a map, if you cannot also find your present location. Right now is a great time and place to start moving toward your dreams. Accept what is, and you're on your way.

Welcome each moment

Welcome each moment, each feeling, each experience as it comes. When you constantly fear or fight whatever is coming next, you become continually stuck where you are.

By welcoming each moment, you begin to move forward. Even if the moment is not exactly what you wanted, welcome it anyway and you become free to move on to whatever is next.

Welcome each moment, whatever it might hold, and you will surely find something of real value in it. There is always a way to move forward, whatever the circumstances may be.

Instead of being weighed down with worry, anger or resentment for what is, put your energy into what can be. Rather than being imprisoned by the shortcomings of a particular moment, set yourself free to live its positive value.

Every moment has its problems, but so what? Welcome it anyway, and rather than dwelling on those problems, you'll already be moving past them. Welcome each moment for the positive possibilities it surely offers, and by so doing you'll begin to transform those possibilities into reality.

Let yourself

Go ahead. Let yourself enjoy the beautiful world around you. Stop fighting life and start flowing with it. Let yourself be full of strength and energy. Let yourself be creative. Let yourself enjoy the moments as they come. It will happen if you let it.

Your own fears and doubts hold you back more than anything else. Your own anger keeps you imprisoned. Your own limiting thoughts conceal an abundance of possibilities. Your worries drain the joy from each moment. Let go of them.

Is that irresponsible? No. The most responsible thing you can do is to live up to your incredible potential. Yes, there are plenty of very real problems in the world. But you don't have to give them any more power than they already have. Let yourself be joyful in spite of them, and your life will be a positive force. Let yourself really live.

Distractions

No matter what you're working to accomplish, you will not get there in a straight line. The phone will ring, people will step into your office, your child will get the chicken pox, bad weather will cause delays, your computer will crash, something new will interest you — you'll repeatedly get knocked off course.

Don't despair. It happens to everyone, all the time. The key to successful achievement is to get quickly back on track. The faster your recovery time, the more progress you'll make.

Accept the fact that you'll get knocked off course on a regular basis. Accept it, and don't waste time or energy complaining about it or feeling sorry for yourself. That just compounds the problem.

Instead, move on past the distraction and re-focus your efforts on your original goal. It is often impossible to prevent distractions, yet you can always prevent them from lingering too long. Move past them as soon as you can, forget about them and get yourself back on course.

It's done

You made a mistake. Or someone else did. Or perhaps something didn't work out the way it should have.

Whatever it was, it has been done. No amount of agonizing or criticizing will change that. To wish that it had never happened, or to pretend that it didn't, would be a waste of good experience.

Find a way to make the best of it. You can't go backward in

time, only forward. And as you go forward, you always have the opportunity to move yourself ahead, regardless of what has happened before.

Make the best of what you have and stop worrying about how you got it. Accept that what's done is done, and focus on the future. Put your energy and effort where they can make a difference, and they will.

Live the adventure

In our desire to make life easy, we can make it far more difficult than it has to be. In our desire to avoid effort, we often make even more effort necessary. In our reluctance to let go, we ultimately lose that which we try to hold.

Think of the things that hold you back. How many of them are the result of your own unwillingness to accept and work through the challenges that are presented to you?

Accept that life is not easy, and it becomes easier. Accept that you must put forth effort, and then the effort isn't so bad. Realize that by letting go of your need to possess, you can have anything.

Today is your opportunity to move forward, to face the challenges, to grow into the person you always knew you could be. Honor the priceless value of your life with the best effort that you can give. Live the adventure that is uniquely yours to fulfill.

Getting it all done

When this day is over, there will be some things that you didn't get done. That's OK. The world will not come to a screeching halt just because every item on your "to do" list didn't get checked off.

Sure, it is important to work diligently, doing what needs to be done. It is also important to enjoy each step along the way. If you postpone your relaxation and enjoyment until after everything is completed, you'll never be able to relax. Because there's always something left to do.

By contrast, when you enjoy each moment as it comes, even when under the pressure of "things to do," then you'll develop a solid confidence that will make your efforts more effective.

What are you giving up, what are you missing out on, in your futile attempt to get "caught up"? Remember, today will be gone soon. Your chance to enjoy it is right now. Relax, and live the golden moments as they move by.

Live as it comes

Too often we give in to the temptation to push the fast forward button, to skip ahead to the next page before we've read the one we're on. As if jumping ahead will somehow make things better, or easier, or more exciting.

The beauty and the joy of life come in living it through. Skipping ahead or jumping back will serve only to cheat you out of the magnificent now.

Live life as it comes. Really live, each moment at a time. String them together, one after the other. Listen to the whole symphony from beginning to end, and savor each passage. Watch the shadows change as the sun rises in the east and works its way across the sky each day. Feel the wind against your face as it grows cooler and then warm.

Take the time to listen, to know, to love those around you.

What a beautiful gift is all of creation and the awareness that you have of it. Drink in every particle.

Float to the top

Do your priorities and commitments empower you or imprison you? If you're feeling overwhelmed and stifled by it all, here's a suggestion: go swimming!

When you try to hold water in your hand, it will soon drain away and you'll lose it. Yet when you immerse yourself in the water, without attempting to hold on to it, letting it flow gently past you, you can enjoy the experience for as long as you wish. If you fight and struggle against the water, you put yourself in danger of drowning. But when you calm down and relax, your natural buoyancy, plus a modest amount of effort, will keep you peacefully afloat no matter what the depth.

Do you find yourself struggling against the very things you set out to achieve? Stop for a moment. Consider the absurdity of that, and the waste of effort which results. Quit thrashing about and permit yourself to calmly float. Your efforts will be infinitely more effective when they're not directed against themselves.

When the stresses and pressures have you feeling like you're drowning, go for a peaceful swim in your mind. Let the depth of your commitment support you rather than sink you.

Acceptance and effectiveness

Acceptance makes you more effective. Effectiveness makes you more accepting. When you accept reality for what it is, then you're better able to change that reality to suit your vision of what it should be.

Likewise, when you know you're effective at changing things, you're much more likely to realistically accept them for what they are. Acceptance and effectiveness build upon each other in an upward spiral.

Acceptance is not giving up or giving in. It is being real. Just because you accept something does not mean you necessarily agree with it. It means that you see it for what it is and understand the implications.

Whatever has happened, has happened. Wherever you are, you are. Whatever has been said or done is over with and there is nothing you can do to change the past. Accept what is, and then know that you can move forward in whatever direction you choose to go, realistically and with your eyes wide open.

Rather than wasting your time and energy fighting against what is, put your efforts into creating what can be.

Forgive and live free

Have you ever carried a grudge for a long time, and then finally let it go? What a sense of relief it can bring when you decide to forgive.

There is a cleansing and refreshing freedom which comes from forgiveness. When you've been hurt, does it make sense to perpetuate the hurt? No, of course not. No one would want to do that. And yet we are often so reluctant to forgive.

Forgiving others does not mean you must trust them or allow them into a position where they can hurt you again. Forgiveness means simply moving on. Forgiveness does not have to make you any less vigilant or any more vulnerable. Forgiveness does not mean that what happened was acceptable. It means that you've chosen to no longer let it hold you back.

There is no real continuing benefit which comes from being a victim. Practice forgiveness and you'll free your spirit to live positively each day, unburdened by the past mistakes of others.

Don't take it personally

Life can sometimes be terribly painful and extremely unfair. When it is, the strongest, most positive and effective response comes from not taking it personally.

Whatever difficulties may come, when you refuse to take them personally you move powerfully beyond the limitations of your own ego. You immediately place yourself at least one level above whatever has happened, and from that vantage point your options are vastly increased.

If someone screams in your face and your reaction is to simply scream back, what have you accomplished? Yet if, instead, you can step back, take your own ego out of the picture, and look objectively at the situation, you can craft and execute a much more effective response.

How do you avoid taking things personally? By keeping in mind that although they may affect you greatly, they do not reflect who you are. Although they have happened to you, they are not an integral part of you. You always have the choice to not take them personally.

That does not mean you do not care. On the contrary, it means that you care enough to put forth your most powerful, effective response.

Admit defeat and enjoy success

Most likely, you have a perfectly legitimate reason for not taking action. You haven't been able to get out and exercise because the weather has been so bad. You can't get any work done on your marketing plan because the phone keeps ringing.

So go ahead and give up. Admit defeat. The weather is not going to improve any time soon. And the phone calls just keep coming. The obstacles that prevent you from taking action are not going away. Admit defeat. And then find a way to take action anyway.

Rather than fighting against something that you cannot change, look for ways to adapt. As long as you're fighting against it, you get a great excuse. But excuses won't help you accomplish anything. So give up the fight, give up the excuse. Go ahead and do what needs to be done. Admit defeat, get it behind you, and then take the actions that will bring you success.

The power of acceptance

Sometimes the best way to free yourself from a burden is to accept it. Much of the destructive essence of any burdensome situation comes from fighting against it. Once you stop fighting, you can start progressing.

Certainly if there is a threat you protect yourself against it. But there is no point in fighting against what already is. When you accept the situation, that is the starting point at which you begin to make the most of it. When you can go beyond acceptance into sincere gratitude, you take on a powerful positive momentum.

In short, accept what is, then find something positive about it. Even the most desperate situation has its positive aspects and possibilities. You'll uncover them only after you've accepted that the situation exists. Acceptance is not surrender. It is the recognition of reality. By clearly seeing what is, by acknowledging and even being grateful, you can move things forward toward the way you would like them to be.

Learning From Life

You can learn

Think of all the things you've learned in your life. When you were born, you did not know how to walk, or talk, or feed yourself. You've learned to read, to count, to travel from place to place. Just in the last few years you've learned how to communicate by e-mail and get access to online information. You've acquired practical wisdom, and mastered complex concepts.

Because of what you've learned, you are not limited to the initial skills and knowledge with which you were born. The things you've learned have enabled you to vastly better understand and interact with the world around you.

You've learned your way around the external terrain. And those same learning skills can be used to overcome the internal obstacles which hold you back. Just as you've learned to read, you can learn to be more focused. Just as you've learned to walk, you can learn to be more disciplined. There's no need to settle for the limited resources you were born with. You can learn.

Pay attention

Pay attention to those who speak with you, and you will tell them more than your words ever could. Pay attention to those you love, and the love will grow. Pay attention to your garden, and it will be full of lush, bright color. Pay attention to your work, and you'll achieve great things. Pay attention to your community, and it will be a wonderful place to live. Pay attention to the direction of your life, and you will find fulfillment.

One of the greatest things you have to give is your attention. Listen, watch, understand, respond. Just think of all the problems which are the result of people not paying attention — to their work, to their children, to their spouses, to where their life is headed, to the society in which they live.

Paying attention is not easy. There are so many distractions. Just like anything else worthwhile, paying attention takes effort and intention. And just like anything else worth doing, the rewards far outweigh the sacrifice. Pay attention, and it will pay you back.

Growing past disappointment

Each disappointment in your life will continue to weigh you down only until you learn and accept what it has to teach you. The moment a disappointment becomes a learning and growing experience is the moment in which it is transformed into a triumph.

The chance to learn from your shortcomings and grow out of your disappointments is one of the richest opportunities you can ever experience. Adversity is a thorough, effective and highly personalized teacher. The powerful lessons learned in the midst of disappointment will stay with you always.

When you can bring yourself to be grateful for your problems you'll begin to harvest their positive value. Life is difficult; out of that difficulty grows meaning and beauty. In each disappointment is the seed of fulfillment. Learn what it has to teach and you'll be moving yourself forward.

Positive lessons

Everyone you meet today has something to teach you. When you feel yourself getting angry, frustrated or impatient with the behavior of others, ask yourself this question. What is this person helping me to learn? Even those who treat you badly can teach you valuable lessons in patience, compassion, forgiveness and other important virtues.

Letting yourself become annoyed or frustrated with others adds no value whatsoever to your life, or to anyone else for that matter. So take a different approach. Challenge yourself to learn from those difficult people and difficult situations.

When an aggressive driver cuts you off, when a slow sales clerk keeps you waiting, when a telemarketer interrupts your evening, look for something to learn from the experience. Redirect the energy of the situation so that something positive comes of it. Look for a way to grow.

Respond to each encounter in a way that will add value to your life and to your world. You'll find that such an approach can quickly make an enormous positive difference.

The strength of weakness

Do you know your weaknesses? Are you willing to admit them and acknowledge them? Are you willing to work on them? What things are holding you back, keeping you from living life exactly as you wish to live?

When you're honest with yourself about your weaknesses, and willing to put some effort into working on them, you have identified a powerful pathway for self improvement.

Imagine a boat with a leak in the hull. Working on the engine might marginally improve its performance, but that really won't do much good because the boat will sink if the leak isn't fixed. A single weakness can sometimes outweigh all the strengths combined.

It's fun and easy to spend time doing the things you're good at. And you certainly want to take full advantage of your strongest skills. Yet usually you can only get marginally better at the things you're already skilled at doing, even with constant practice. However, when you set out to work on your weaknesses, the effort can produce dramatic, leveraged results. Identify your weaknesses, put some effort into them, and you can make a tremendous positive difference.

Experience

Others can guide you, teach you, and encourage you. Yet what you truly know is whatever you experience for yourself.

When you understand and appreciate the true value of experience, then every experience indeed becomes valuable. The good times and the not-so-good times all bring with them the golden treasure of experience.

Be willing to live through whatever life sends your way, and you will grow stronger with each passing moment. Be thankful for the opportunity to experience whatever may be happening, and the experience you gain will serve you well.

You are more capable, more knowledgeable, more effective than you've ever been before. And with each new experience, that positive and valuable growth continues.

Delight each day in the experience of life. Treasure it, learn from it, live it and use every moment to reach ever higher.

The power of understanding

So many problems could be solved or avoided if more people would make the simple effort to understand and appreciate the perspective of others. So many opportunities and possibilities would be greatly enhanced if those involved would seek to better understand each other.

Empathy and a depth of understanding are not just nice things to do. They are powerful strategic tools that will greatly enhance your effectiveness. The better you know and understand the other person's perspective, the more successful you'll be at dealing with that person.

Fortunes have been built because someone understood what people truly wanted. Fortunes have been lost by those who didn't understand.

In our hurry-up world, too many people don't even take notice of the other people around them, much less acknowledge or seek to understand them. That is unfortunate and ultimately takes a costly toll.

Take the time to notice, to consider, to understand and appreciate the people around you. It is one of the most powerful ways to enhance your own life. You don't have to agree with the other person, just seek to understand. It can make a major positive difference for everyone concerned.

I don't know

One of the smartest things you can do is to admit when you don't know something. The most intelligent people are not those who purport to know it all. The most intelligent people are those who have a realistic awareness of what they know and, just as importantly, what they don't know.

Some people foolishly pretend to know things when in fact they don't. It sometimes serves their pride, yet in the end such behavior is completely self defeating.

Admitting you don't know something is the first step in learning it. No one can possibly know everything. There is no shame in not knowing.

There is so much you can learn when you admit to yourself and others that you don't know. It is far better to admit you don't know, than to proceed with missing or incomplete knowledge. Have the courage to say "I don't know" and then make the commitment to find out.

Criticism

Welcome criticism just as you would welcome praise. No matter what you might say or do there will always be those who are anxious to criticize.

Generally, it is a waste of time to refute the criticism of others. When you speak the truth and act with integrity, you will be proven right in the end. So if the criticism is unjustified, it will be discredited with or without your defense. If the criticism is indeed justified, then your best course is to heed it rather than to refute it.

Criticism can hurt you only if you let it. Put honest thought, effort, competence and commitment into your undertakings, and the criticism of others will not matter. The negativity of your critics is their problem, not yours.

Living the Wonder of It All

Focus on going forward in pursuit of your goals. Let your critics enjoy the perverse pleasure of their negativity, while you move right on past them.

Perceptions

What if your limitations were all an illusion? What if you were being held back, not by your circumstances, but by your mind? Though it is easy to recognize the perceptual bias of another, your own perceptions are more difficult to distinguish from reality.

In many ways the world you see is of your own making. Consider what that could mean. The obstacles you perceive may not really be there if you could get your mind beyond them. The limitations against which you struggle could be gone the instant you change your viewpoint.

What may appear to be cold, hard, immutable reality could melt away and be transformed by the power of your own perceptions. Though it is foolish to ignore reality, it is tragic to be frozen by it.

What if you could change the world and didn't know it? What if you suddenly figured it out? Look beyond the obvious. Look beyond your assumptions. Step outside the window of your perceptions and marvel at the vastness of possibility.

Step back

Imagine that you could step back away from yourself, a distance of four or five feet — far enough to be completely detached and yet near enough to carefully observe.

What would you see? How would you appear to yourself?

Would you be pleased with what you observed? What advice would you be anxious to convey?

Try looking objectively at yourself from a bit of a distance, right now. For a moment, view yourself as you would view another person, with a measure of objectivity and detachment. Consider how your actions and your priorities look from the outside. Watch how you spend the precious moments that make up each day. Not only will you find opportunities for improvement. You'll also spot many superb possibilities. It will help you to gain a new and valuable perspective on yourself.

You already know how it is from the inside looking out. Try getting on the outside, looking in. You'll see the world in a new and positive way.

Listen

You can learn a lot from listening. Unfortunately, very few people actually do it. When the other person is talking, most of us are so busy trying to think of what we will say next that we don't fully appreciate what is being said.

Conversation is not a contest. It is an exchange. When you fail to listen well, you shortchange yourself. The next time you listen to someone else, try really listening. Seek to understand their point of view, even if you don't agree with it. There is always something you can learn.

When you truly listen, you won't have to worry about what you say next. Whatever you say will pale in comparison to the positive impression you make from listening attentively.

Listen and learn. Listen with respect. Listen, and gain the rapport and respect of others. Listening is easy if you will just decide to do it. Add power and effectiveness to your communication — listen, really listen.

Have you learned yet?

Mistakes are great teachers. The lessons you learn from them are very specific, compelling and highly appropriate to your own unique situation. Your mistakes are custom-designed lessons, made just for you. Mistakes are very persistent teachers. If you fail to learn from them, they'll keep coming back, stronger each time, until you do.

Learning from your mistakes is more than just an intellectual exercise. When you've truly learned from a mistake, it will change your actions or behavior. When you realize that you've made a mistake, consider this. Have you learned its lesson yet? Are you doing something differently as a result?

If so, then you've made the very best of the situation and used the mistake to your advantage. You've learned, you've grown, and you've become more effective. A successful life is built in large part by trial and error. Give your mistakes the respect they deserve, learn what they have to teach, and they will propel you forward.

Living With a Flexible, Creative Open Mind

An exquisite contradiction

You are the same person you were yesterday, and yet you are also more than you have ever been before. You are changing on a moment by moment basis, and yet at some level you remain the person you have always been.

Stop for a moment and consider what a beautiful paradox it is. You constantly move through life, learning, growing, experiencing, becoming, while all the time continuing to be you.

You can embrace change without abandoning the absolute, fundamental values which provide a solid foundation for your existence, your purpose, your fulfillment. You can stand firm while at the same time learning, adjusting, accepting and adapting.

Part of moving successfully forward is your ability to stay firmly anchored to who you are and to what you know is always true. And part of maintaining a strong sense of who you are is your willingness to change for the better.

You are fixed and you are flexible. It is an exquisite contradiction. Learn to see the value in those things which do not change, and also in those things which can be changed for the better. They both have their place, they both have their value, and they both are yours to use in living a life of meaning and fulfillment.

Adapt and prosper

When conditions change, some people become immobilized by worry. Other people complain. Still others make the changing conditions into an excuse for not taking action. What do successful people do when conditions change? Successful people adapt. That's what makes them consistently successful.

When conditions change, suddenly there can be plenty of reasons to give up. Suddenly there can be plenty of perfectly understandable justifications for not moving forward. Suddenly there can be an abundance of excuses for failure.

And yet, when conditions change there are also great opportunities. Some people will have the confidence to recognize those opportunities and act upon them. Someday everyone will say those people were lucky, that they were in the right place at the right time.

The truth is, when you're willing and able to adapt, you're always in the right place at the right time. Those who recognize that fact and take advantage of it by adapting in a positive way to changing conditions will be very fortunate indeed.

Another approach

When one approach is not working to reach the desired goal, that's not a reason to abandon the goal. Instead, it is time to devise another approach. Sometimes the objective and the means to that objective become so intertwined that it is difficult to imagine one without the other. Yet there are many different ways to reach any particular goal, given enough persistence and creativity.

That's why, for those who are able to consistently get things done, there is no such thing as failure. There are only approaches which have been proven ineffective.

There is a way to achieve whatever you desire, even when you've already fallen short of the mark. There is a way to do it. That way may not be obvious. It may well require some skillful, creative thinking. It's there, though. Learn from each attempt, learn from each approach and you'll surely discover one that works spectacularly.

Differing opinions

If you listen only to those with whom you already agree, there's only so much you can learn. Take the time and effort to consider other points of view. Often you can learn the most from those with whom you disagree, if you respect them enough to listen and truly consider what they have to say.

Be careful not to get trapped by labels. Just because someone disagrees with you about one thing, does not necessarily mean that person will disagree with you about everything.

You can find value in the thinking and opinions of others without compromising your own convictions. Each person with whom you interact has a unique perspective. In that perspective is a golden treasure just waiting to be uncovered.

Anyone who has an opinion can perpetuate a disagreement, but what does that accomplish? Rather than looking for a reason to disagree, look for value in all the differing points of view which you encounter. Only when you're confident enough to acknowledge that you don't know it all will you be able to grow in knowledge and wisdom.

Living the Wonder of It All

Beyond reason

Reason will serve you well but reason alone cannot sustain your spirit. Some of the best things in life are unreasonable. Love and beauty exist largely outside of reason. The heart embraces things which the most reasonable mind does not even consider.

Be reasonable, yet do not limit yourself to being reasonable. On a regular basis, let yourself go beyond reason. There's no need to reject reason. Just add to it, and most every aspect of your life will benefit.

In the midst of suffering and pain, hope may indeed be completely unreasonable. Even so, it has the power to sustain and strengthen beyond all reasonable expectations. In the face of continued setbacks and disappointments, perseverance may seem entirely unreasonable. Yet such ill-reasoned diligence has often resulted in great discoveries, creations and fortunes.

Reason is based on the things you already know. Beyond reason there is much you can learn. Seek to know the unknown. Spend some time being creatively and positively unreasonable. Regularly nurture your spirit as well as your mind. Make excursions outside the box of reason and you'll return with positively energized spirit.

Surprises

Every day will be full of surprises. Some will be pleasant, some even joyful, others will be disappointing, sad or even tragic. Accept that they will come with or without your worry and anxiety.

Plan and anticipate, but don't worry or fret. It gets you nothing. Just do. Spend your energy and time creatively and productively, not on anger, envy or worry.

Do your very best without being obsessed about getting it perfect. Treat people with respect and sincerity without being too concerned about what they think of you. Be your true self without fear of embarrassment. Accept what is, and go from there to what you wish to be.

You have plenty of time, energy and resources available to you, more than enough to build the life you desire. Take care not to fritter them away on the meaningless, trivial things.

The surprises will come. Take them in stride. Be prepared, but don't be afraid. Live each moment with positive purpose and your days will be incredibly rich.

Create

Creativity does not get used up. In fact, the more you exercise your creativity, the more you have of it. Creativity feeds upon itself. What may at first seem like a small, insignificant idea, can grow into something substantial when you let the creativity continue to flow.

A magnificent painting begins with a single brush stroke, creatively applied. One creative act leads to another, and soon you have a masterpiece. We often imagine creativity as being on a grand scale, and yet it is in the grainy texture of life that true creativity occurs.

Anyone, anywhere can be creative. It's just a matter of opening the mind, stepping outside the comfortable box of your limitations, then putting into form and action the original thoughts which come to you.

Create, and then create again. Allow your creativity to build upon its own energy, into something of unique value and beauty.

Uncertainty

Something unexpected will happen today. No matter how thoroughly you have planned each moment, something you did not plan for will come along.

You can choose to let it annoy you and disrupt you. You can worry and fret about things not going the way you planned. Or, you can accept that every day will have some uncertainly, and then adapt to whatever comes along.

Though uncertainty can be annoying or even frightening, just think of all the good things it has brought you — that valuable new idea that came to you out of the blue, or that great new friend you didn't expect to meet.

The future is uncertain. Sure, we need to plan in detail and then follow our plans. Yet we must also realize and accept that few things will turn out exactly the way we had in mind.

If you curse and fight uncertainty, it will ruin your plans. Instead, learn to accept and adapt to changing conditions, and you'll find that things begin to turn out even better than you had planned.

Flexible focus

To achieve anything worthwhile, it is important to stay focused and to avoid being sidetracked by the many distractions which inevitably come your way. And yet it is also important to stay flexible, so you can adjust, adapt to, and take advantage of changing situations.

How do you stay focused without being too rigid, and flexible without being too limp? By having a clear understanding of what is important.

Being clearly focused on the ultimate goal does not require that you be unyielding on every detail. Success comes from standing firm on the important, big-picture issues, while staying flexible on the little things which, in the end, don't really matter one way or another.

Great achievements demand a healthy balance between firm resolve and open-minded flexibility. Know clearly, precisely, exactly what you wish to accomplish, and be adaptable enough to turn every situation toward that purpose. Just because you occasionally leave the path, does not mean you must forsake the destination. Stay focused, be flexible, and get yourself there.

Living With Courage

What are you so afraid of?

The next time you feel anxiety, frustration, anger or despair, ask yourself — what are you so afraid of? Negative reactions are almost always based on fear.

Many fears are useful and even essential. Other fears are not. Yet no matter how realistic or unrealistic a fear may be, it is always helpful to know what that fear is.

Why waste effort avoiding your fears, when you can use that energy to confront them? Look directly at your fears, and you've taken the first step toward getting past them.

Seek to cure the problem rather than just the symptom. Avoid hiding behind your negative reactions. Save yourself a lot of anguish. If there's something that causes you fear, do something about it.

Take the plunge

If you're not a little bit apprehensive, then you're not reaching high enough.

To move forward, you must put yourself on the line. That means going beyond your comfortable routine. Your abilities increase only when you regularly strive to go beyond them. Your effectiveness improves only when challenges pull you beyond your limits.

That sinking feeling you get, when moving into uncharted territory, is a precursor to success. Preparation and planning are vital, and confidence is essential. Yet alone they do not bring accomplishment. At some point, you must take the plunge. You'll never be as ready as you wanted to be. It will never be as comfortable as you'd like it to be.

Do it anyway, and make the commitment to give it your best. Challenge undertaken with sincerity of purpose, will build in you the strength needed to prevail.

Live in courage

You've done many courageous things. Just getting out of bed in the morning takes some degree of courage. And you've gone way past that.

Think of a time in your life when you were particularly courageous, a time when you were especially creative, persistent, focused or adventurous. Consider that you are still the same person even now. Certainly circumstances have changed since then, and you have changed as well. Yet that capacity for courage is still with you.

Connect yourself with that courage and put your life into it. You have it, there's no doubt. It is there, waiting to move you forward. Let yourself live in it.

Though the world is often harsh, there are boundless opportunities all around you. And you have the courage to make the most of them. Gather the circumstances of your life and let that courage infuse them, so that everything becomes an opportunity for moving forward. Live in courage and make life great.

Risk and reward

In order to win, you must be willing to lose. If you spend your life afraid of failure, failure is exactly what you'll get. Without the possibility of failure, there is no possibility for success.

From the moment you are born, life is risky. It doesn't matter where you live, what kind of work you do, or how much money you have, there are always risks. You cannot escape them — emotional risks, physical risks, financial risks, social risks. It is impossible to live without risk. What you must do is learn how to make the risks pay.

If would be foolish indeed to take risks that offered no possibility of reward. And yet it is just as foolish to let the fear of failure prevent you from taking action. Consider this. You've made it this far in spite of the risks, and along the way you've learned a thing or two. You've probably had a few failures, and they certainly weren't fatal.

So whatever you want, go for it! Life is risky anyway, so seek out the risks that bring the greatest rewards. Put yourself on the line, and then give all you have to the effort. Stand up, stand out and achieve your dream.

Turn on your courage

Even on the most difficult days there is hope. The worst that could possibly happen cannot even come close to the good that already is. The whole world could crumble around you and still there would be the very real presence of joy and fulfillment in your life.

The best things you have, you cannot ever lose. The most important things can never be taken from you no matter what tragedy may befall you.

And therein lies the strength to attempt anything. You truly cannot fail, so you might as well succeed in the most spectacular fashion. Yes, you will stumble and there will be pain, but it can never equal the joy of which you're capable. Even though no one may catch you when you fall, the minute you hit bottom there will be endless ways to start climbing again.

Act strong because you are strong. Go confidently forward knowing that even the very worst days are still full on wonder and exciting possibility. You have a great life to be lived. Turn on your courage and make it happen.

Fear of criticism

Think for a moment how silly it is to live in fear of criticism. If you're doing what you know to be right, what possible reason could you have to fear the criticism of others?

Are you concerned that the comments and opinions of others will somehow damage your self esteem or self image? Are you afraid of speaking your mind or taking action because you might get your feelings hurt?

If you really want to improve your self esteem, stop allowing other people to be responsible for it. Instead, create something of value. Make a positive difference. Pats on the back are nice, but in the end the thing that will truly make you feel good about yourself is to accomplish something worthwhile.

Find valuable feedback in the criticism of others. Realize that it can't hurt you, that it actually can help. Go forward with the confidence of knowing that you're truly making a difference, and you will indeed.

Fear of failure

Are you afraid to fail, so afraid that you don't even make the attempt? When you think about it, that really makes no sense. By not even making an attempt, you are guaranteeing failure. So the fear of failure leads straight to certain failure.

Do you feel fear? Great! Examine that fear. Look for the message it is intended to convey. Fear can make you more aware. It can give you increased energy. It can prepare you to overcome difficult challenges. Fear can harness your resources like nothing else can.

Your fear is there to help you move effectively forward, not to hold you back. Let it teach you. Let it prepare you. Don't let it stop you. When fear is holding you back, look closely at that fear and you'll find a way to move forward.

The only lasting failure is the failure to act. If you do make the attempt and fail to get the desired result, learn from it and give it another go. You cannot fail when you continue to take action.

Venture out

There are a lot of terrible things that might happen today. They might happen, but they probably won't. And yet too often the apprehension over those things that might be, unlikely as they are, holds us back from the great things that very well could be. And ironically, what ends up happening is the very worst thing that could possibly happen — nothing at all.

Though there are risks in every moment, they are far outweighed by the positive possibilities. For every difficulty that might befall you, there are a dozen opportunities waiting to be seized.

Boldly venture out today and every day. Live fully the miraculous life with which you're blessed. The joys are yours to experience when you have the courage and faith to participate. Take a deep breath. Realize that there's a whole, wonderful world just waiting for you to relish. Be a part of it. Focus on the great things that could be, and delight in making them happen.

Confidence

You are a unique and valuable person, no matter what. No error in judgment, no embarrassment, no pain, no setback can take away the inherent value of who you are and who you can be.

Certainly you want to be the best you can be. And the way to do that is by being confident of who you are. If you let every little thing, and even every big thing, get to you, your confidence can quickly be eroded. The more you worry, the more reason you'll have to worry.

There's no reason to get caught in such a downward spiral. Instead, always keep in mind that no circumstance, no setback, no turn of events can ever have the power on its own to change your value as a person.

Every life will have its share of unfortunate situations, but that is certainly no reason to cower in fear or to become consumed with anxiety. Rather, you have every reason to move confidently forward. Whatever life may take from you will never be able to deplete the good and valuable things you have to give.

You've made it

You can handle whatever life gives you. You did it yesterday, and the day before. You've done it all your life, and it has brought you to where you are today. Somehow, in some way, you have successfully made your way through every challenge, to arrive at this point in life, right here, right now.

Every day for as long as you can remember you've faced challenges, you've solved problems, and you have worked your way through the obstacles that blocked your path. You have proved to yourself and to the world that you are resourceful, that you are effective, that you can propel yourself to where you want to be.

Nothing yet has stopped you. You've proven that you can handle the challenges. Don't stop now. Have the courage to go for what you truly want. Sure, the task looks daunting. Sure, there are hurdles to be overcome. Yet that's what you're so good at doing. You've made it here, and you can make it anywhere you want to go.

Beyond doubt

The most reliable and effective way to conquer your doubts is with action. Whatever you're seeking to accomplish or overcome, there will continue to be some doubt in your mind that you can do it, until you actually step forward and begin to do it.

The steps you take at first may be small, and seemingly insignificant. Yet those first steps are vital. They are the ones which begin to build your positive momentum. Those first steps are the ones which start to erase the most persistently lingering doubts.

From the very first effort, you'll begin to replace doubt and fear with courage and confidence. And as you do that you'll be paving the way for bigger, more ambitious steps forward. In this way, your positive actions and confidence will feed on each other to create an ever-expanding forward momentum. Soon the doubts will be left far behind.

As soon as you begin to take action, your doubts and fears will start to lose their power. Doubts can often seem overwhelming, yet your real and focused efforts will make those doubts less and less real, until they finally disappear completely.

Connect with courage

Courage begins when you realize that you have it. Courage grows stronger the more it is used.

Everyone has fears, and everyone has the capacity for courage. Courage requires no special skill or training. Courage is what happens when you take action in spite of your fears. Courage comes when you are willing to learn from your fears, to make prudent adjustments based on what those fears tell you, and to be pushed forward by those fears rather than held back by them.

Take the first courageous step forward, and the second step will easily follow. By the time you get to the fifth or sixth step, it starts to become automatic as the power of your courage becomes clearly evident.

Courage is a choice which cannot be denied to you by anyone other than yourself. No person or circumstance can prevent you from making use of your courage. It is yours when you choose to tap into its power.

Connect with your courage and discover what an enormous difference it can make in your life and your world.

Living With Action

The spirit is willing, but...

Does this sound familiar? You know what you need to do. You know you need to be more disciplined, more focused, more positive, more industrious. Yet there's a big difference between knowing what to do and putting it into practice. How do you get yourself to actually step forward and take the necessary action?

The problem is often that long term goals conflict with short term desires. You'd like to lose weight someday, but you want that bowl of ice cream right now. What's the way around this trap? Simply get your short term desires to support your long term goals.

Find something you can do right now, something which is completely and totally enjoyable in its own right, and which also brings long term benefits. Then enjoy it. Get hooked on it. When you're not doing it, think about how much you wish you could be doing it.

Here's an example. I get up before sunrise every morning and go for a one-hour walk. It is quiet, peaceful, cool, invigorating and extremely enjoyable. It gets each day off to a great start. The benefits are immediate and positive. Just thinking about how good it feels is enough to get me out of bed at that early hour. Plus, it supports my long term goal of staying physically fit.

For every long term goal that you truly want to achieve, there is some highly enjoyable and immediately compelling way to pursue that goal, right now. Figure out what it is, let yourself truly delight in doing it, and you're unstoppable!

The joy of effort

Nothing can match the joy and satisfaction which come from sustained and effective effort. Every person, at some level, has a desire to make a difference. Getting things done, making things happen, creating positive value though effort is a powerful and proven way to make that difference.

Yet all too often we go out of our way to seek comfort and convenience while avoiding as much effort as possible. We make the tragic assumption that "the good life" is defined by an absence of effort, when in fact the opposite is true. There's nothing more empty than a life devoted to leisure.

Fill your days with honest and effective effort. Make a difference in a positive way and your rewards will be great. Experience the abundance of joy which comes from making things happen and getting things done.

Dig in

Even the most modest effort can be enough to change your momentum from negative to positive. But why settle for just a modest effort? When life seems overwhelming, dig in and go to work. Just because there is much to be done, is no reason to give up. To the contrary, the more burdensome the challenges, the more of a difference you can make.

Dig in. Tackle one task, and then another. Keep going. You're making progress. Momentum is on your side when you make the effort to make a difference.

Welcome the exhilaration of confronting the challenges which face you. Solve problems, plan, organize, build, create value. Make the world a better place in your own unique way. What could possibly be more fulfilling? Live the adventures that those overwhelming challenges bring. Dig in, go to work, and make it happen.

Building blocks

A tiny droplet of water is soft and relatively harmless. If it were to fall on your head from out of the sky, you probably would not even notice. Yet when enough tiny, soft droplets are grouped together, they can form a large and powerful storm, with the force to topple buildings and alter the landscape.

Big things are made out of little things. To gain control over the big things, you must control the little things, over and over again. Small moments of time don't seem like much. They come and go largely without notice. Yet, put enough of them together, focused on a clearly defined objective, and they can bring truly awesome results.

It is easy to set one brick on top of another. Do it often enough and you have a strong, solid wall. It is easy to pick up the phone and make a single prospecting call. Do it often enough and you'll build a massive customer base. It is easy to put a few thoughts on paper. Do it often enough and you've written a masterpiece.

Every achievement is built, one small step at a time. Plan your steps. Then take them, one after another, and you'll get yourself there.

Hope

Hope will keep you going if you don't let it hold you back.

For hope to be of value, it must be put into action. Hope cannot be a substitute for action. If we hope that things will get better, and then use that hope as a reason to avoid the effort that would make them better, what has hope achieved?

We can act with hope, yet it is not enough to depend on hope alone. Indeed, we must respect our hopes by making a commitment to them — a solid commitment of time, energy and action. Hope must not become an excuse, but rather an inspiration.

Have hope, and be careful not to take refuge in it. Live each moment with hope, while knowing that you cannot prosper by hope alone. You'll find power in your hopes. Put that power into action. Hope for the best, and then do what it takes to make that a reality.

Effort

Behind every fortune, is someone who has labored long into the night to make it real. Behind every important discovery, is a person who regularly grew weary searching for it.

Behind the magnificent work of art is an artist who spent hour after hour, month after month toiling at tasks that were not so magnificent.

Take heart. Your effort cannot help but pay off. The fact is, your effort is the payoff. The fortune, the discovery, the work of art are mere tokens of the achievement. The real achievement is in the achieving. The real value is in the doing.

Sincere, focused effort makes your life rich, even as you do it. Otherwise, why would we put so much value on the artifacts which it produces? Make the effort. The biggest reward is in the doing.

Stop trying

Trying can be very trying. It's often the case that the harder you try, the less you get accomplished.

Why is that? When you're trying there is the assumption of failure. If you heard someone say "I'm trying to get the report finished on time" how would you interpret it? Would you have confidence that the report would be ready on time? Probably not. More likely, you'd assume that it wouldn't be.

Stop trying and start doing. Trying will give you excuses. Doing will get you results. There's a big difference, and it's mostly in your attitude. Forget about trying. Trying is barely more effective than idle wishing. Remove the word "trying" from your vocabulary, and notice how much that simple step clarifies your activities. You're either doing it or you're not. You're either taking action or you're not.

Stop trying and get going.

You know

It's easier to think that you've missed a big opportunity, than it is to take advantage of that opportunity. It's easier to think that you've done all you can, than it is to make just a little more effort. It's easier to think that you know all the answers, than it is to learn something new. It's easier to think that things won't get any better, than it is to put forth the effort to make them better.

Living the Wonder of It All   83

It's easier to think, than it is to do. And way too many people choose the easy way out. But not you.

You know better. You know there is plenty of opportunity, if only you will work for it. You know that just a little extra effort can make the difference between a fortune and a failure. You know that the smartest people are those who have the most to learn. You know that things will get better when you are committed to making them better.

You know how life works. You know what you want. You know you can do it. Sure, it's easy to think that you can't or you won't. But you know what to do. You know, and you will. Today would be good, right now would be better.

One step

No matter how long you've been walking north, in just a single step you can be walking south. What does it take to turn your life around? Just one step.

You are one step away from eating a healthier diet, one step away from being a better parent, one step away from improving your finances, one step away from becoming more skilled in your work, one step away from a more fulfilling relationship.

One minute from now, your worst problems can be behind you, instead of in front of you. In a single step, your best day can be yet to come, rather than long ago in the past. In an instant, your negative energy can be redirected toward making a positive difference.

Just one step can change your momentum, and start you in whatever direction you truly want to go.

Living the Wonder of It All

There's always tomorrow

I really should finish that report... but there's always tomorrow. I need to start working out more often... but there's always tomorrow. I really should return her phone call... but there's always tomorrow.

There's always tomorrow. And that is precisely the problem. If you put something off until tomorrow, guess what? There will always be another tomorrow, and another and another, ready and waiting for you to continue procrastinating.

While there is always another tomorrow, there will never be another opportunity to make the most of today. Once today is over, it is history. No amount of regret or sorrow or excuses will change it.

Today becomes a done deal in just a few hours. Right now is your golden opportunity to make it count.

Act quickly

Problems don't go away by themselves, but opportunities do. If you wait for problems to just disappear, they usually get more serious. And if you dawdle while opportunity is knocking, it soon will leave and knock on someone else's door.

If something needs doing, get right on it. Be patient, yes, but do so while taking action. If you're reluctant to do something that needs to be done, consider that it will only get worse, the longer you wait.

How would you like to have super-human strength? Act quickly, and you can solve 10 problems with the same effort it would take to deal with just one problem which has been avoided and grown to serious proportions. The faster you take action, the more effective you can be.

Certainly you don't want to jump without looking, but as soon as you've decided what needs to be done, get busy doing it. Time is your most precious resource and the less time you wait to get started, the less time you'll spend doing it. Get on it right now!

Complaining

Complaining about a situation is a poor substitute for doing something about it. Complaining might give you the feeling that you're taking action, but in reality it is a technique for avoiding action. We often complain as a way to resolve an issue in our own minds, yet complaints resolve nothing.

Consider what you would do if complaining was not an option — if there was no such thing, or if it was illegal. What if there was no one to whom you could complain? What would you do?

You would take action. You would really, truly resolve the problem, instead of simply speculating and griping about it.

If you find yourself complaining frequently, particularly if it's about the same thing, that's a solid indication that you need to stop complaining and start doing. It's easy to see that your complaints have accomplished nothing. So what's the point? Instead, pretend that complaining is not an option, and you'll find yourself compelled to take positive action.

Anyone can

Anyone who flips on a light switch will cause the lights to turn on. Anyone who shifts an automobile into gear and presses on the accelerator pedal, will cause the car to move forward. Anyone who takes the steps necessary to build a successful business, will do so.

Achieving results is a matter of putting forth the necessary effort. Anyone can achieve any result by making the specific efforts required to reach that result.

Make the same efforts as a winner, and you will have the same results. Take the necessary sequence of steps, and you'll arrive at the destination of your choice.

It really doesn't matter who you are, or where you came from, or what disappointments you've experienced in the past. Any achievement, no matter how small or how grand, is a simple cause-and-effect proposition. Make the right effort and you'll get the desired result.

Act like it

Do you wish to be financially independent? Then act like it. Do you wish to be a loving parent or spouse? Then act like it. Do you wish to be in great physical shape? Then act like it. Is it your desire to be a leader, an innovator, to be creative, to be respected, to be taken seriously? Then act like it!

Wishes are empty without action. The way you act will determine the reality of your life. People who act in a certain way will win on the playing field. People who act in other ways will make a lot of money, or have great relationships, or become leaders in their community. It is not all that difficult to see and understand which actions lead to which results.

The path that leads from the desire to the fulfillment is clear and undeniable. It demands intentional, focused and sustained action. You are just as capable of following that path as anyone else. Whatever you wish to be, or have, or do or experience, make a commitment to act like it and it will happen.

You are what you do

Your beliefs and values are not what you say they are. Your beliefs and values are what you do. Your actions communicate with a veracity that is difficult to deny or ignore.

Success and achievement require more than intention. They require a substance of action. You are not necessarily what you appear to be or what you would like to be. You are what you do.

Your actions reveal your true commitments and priorities. They create the substance of your life. Your actions make all the difference in the world, and they are under your control. The quality of your life is determined by the quality and consistency of your actions.

Each day, take positive action like your life depends on it. Because it does.

Work to be done

The fact that there is much work still to be done, many obstacles still to be overcome, is no reason to be dismayed. Because the moments will come, you will fill them with effort and value, and life will grow increasingly richer as a result.

The assumption that effort is something to be avoided is simply not true. Wishing for a life free of challenges is wishing for something you really would not want if you ever got it.

Look back at where you've come from and you will understand. You'll see that the times which have brought the most value and richness to your life were the times which demanded the most of you.

Find joy in the challenges, in the efforts, in the living and in the giving. The moments when much is asked of you, are the moments when much is given to you.

What an incredible, priceless opportunity it is to be able to work, to learn, to grow, to accomplish and to drink in all the richness along the way. There is always work to be done and there is indeed no better way for things to be.

Creating Value

Wish list

Imagine this. You wake up one morning and quickly discover that everything you wish for will magically and instantly appear in front of you. You wish for a brand new sports car and poof, it appears in your garage. You wish for a slim, muscular physique and poof, you have it. This is fun, you think.

You wish for a billion dollars in your bank account and suddenly it is there. Then you realize you don't really need the money because you no longer must buy anything. You wish for a new computer, a puppy, a giant house, a loving companion. They all appear instantly. Physical manifestations of your desires begin to surround you.

After a while it becomes overwhelming. Even the most casual thought causes a "poof" and another artifact appears on top of the growing pile. Suddenly it gets very boring and quite senseless. What good is all this stuff, anyway? You soon grow to resent your desires, because they are filling your life with useless junk. You cannot escape them.

You finally wish to not have this power anymore, and that wish, too, is granted. Instantly, all the new stuff disappears and you are left with only the experience and a little more wisdom.

It all gives you a profound new appreciation for the value of effort. You realize that your desires are not fulfilled by the things you desire, but rather by the person you become in the process of following those desires. When you could have had anything in the world, the life you have right now — with all its struggles and frustrations — is what you selected over everything else.

Be necessary

Success comes from making yourself necessary. It does not come from making a nuisance of yourself, nor from making people feel sorry for you, nor from taking advantage of others. In whatever arena you seek success, you will attain it by making a useful and substantial contribution.

What are you doing right now to make yourself necessary? How much of yourself do you put into your work, into your life? True, lasting achievement requires effort on your part. You may be able to lie, cheat or steal your way to a big bank account, but you cannot steal true success and fulfillment. It must be earned. It must come from you. It must come from making your own unique, positive contribution to the world.

You're a special individual, and the best thing you can do with your uniqueness is to make it available to others. Make yourself necessary. Make a difference. Your own life is the most blessed when the most others are blessed by it

Giving and taking

Whatever you seek to acquire, the most reliable way to get it is by giving, rather than by taking. To obtain wealth, give value. To be happy, make other people happy. To truly learn, teach others. To be loved, give love. To be respected, act with respect toward others.

When you attempt to take what you want, you'll be met with suspicion, barbed wire and guard dogs. By contrast, when you give of yourself, you encounter little or no resistance.

Sincerely seek to give, to provide value, to make a difference, and people will line up to support you. Every person alive, no matter how sincerely selfless and altruistic they may be, is concerned in some way with their own self interest — if they weren't they would stop breathing and die. You can be sure that anyone with whom you come in contact is influenced to some degree by their own self interest. However, you cannot be sure that they are the least bit interested in you.

That being the case, you're considerably more likely to achieve your own success when you champion the self interest of others. It's as close as you can get to a sure thing.

Who can you help?

Think of everyone around you — in your family, your school, your office, your community, your country, your world. Who can you help? How can you help them?

What value do you have to impart to others? Answer that question, and it will lead you to wherever you want to go.

Do not think that you have nothing of value to offer. You most certainly do. Your job is to find what that is, to discover who you can help, and how you can help them. The value you have to offer is most likely a mixture of your knowledge, your skills, your opinions, your interests, your likes and dislikes, the people you know, and the experiences you've lived through.

Help others enjoy prosperity, and you will become wealthy. Help others to be truly happy, and you will be filled with joy. Teach to others, and you will learn. No matter who you are or

Living the Wonder of It All

how doggedly life has beat you down, you have something to offer, something that will make your life shine.

Who can you help? What can you do to make a difference?

Invest in kindness

A snide remark gains you nothing, yet costs you much. A selfish act brings no lasting value, yet it attracts the enduring resentment of others. A kind word, on the other hand, costs you nothing. And it can bring about a lifetime of value.

What if, just once each day, you were to stop yourself before making a cruel remark and replace it with a sincere word of encouragement? Such a thing would cost you absolutely nothing, and yet it would bring real, positive value to your life and your world.

Cruelty is a waste of precious time and energy. Kindness is an investment which pays endless dividends.

If you desire a life of value, then do the things which bring true value, as often as you can. Fill your moments with kindness, and fill your world with value.

Ambition or arrogance?

Too many people confuse ambition with arrogance, and then wonder why it fails them.

The distinctions between ambition and arrogance are sometimes subtle, yet critical. From a distance, the two can appear to be the same. However, their results are worlds apart.

Ambition is expecting the best of yourself. Arrogance is believing you are better than others. Ambition is the desire to make a difference. Arrogance is the belief that you're indispensable. Ambition is doing whatever it takes to accomplish what you know you deserve. Arrogance is thinking that the world owes you something, and doing what you can to take it. Ambition is disciplined and assertive. Arrogance is pushy. Ambition is responsible and respectful. Arrogance is destructive and disdainful.

Are you driven by ambition or arrogance? Arrogance will drive you into the ground. Ambition will drive you to the top.

What is best

Sure, it's a lot easier to think you've already missed the big opportunity than it is to make that opportunity work for you. And it's easier to assume you've done all you can than it is to put in just a little more effort to make absolutely sure.

It's much easier to tell yourself that you know all the answers than it is to go through the effort of learning something new. And it's much easier to talk about doing something than it is to actually get busy and do it.

But the easy way is not usually the best way. The best way is to do what you know is right. Do you know what is right? Of course you do.

You know that opportunity is always there for those who are willing to put in the work that it requires. You know that often your extra efforts can make the difference between spectacular success and mediocrity.

You know that the smartest people are those who have the courage to admit what they don't know. And you know that it takes more than just talk to make things happen.

You've seen how life works, and you've seen what makes the difference between success and failure. Keep that in mind when making your own choices, every moment, every day. Enjoy the benefits that come from choosing what is right and what is best.

Really live

Imagine a sparkling, blue sea, filled with life and color and beauty. Now think for a moment about how you can most fully experience it.

If you try to take it for yourself and keep what you have taken for yourself and no one else, all you end up with is a bucket of salty water. Yet when you let go of your need to possess, and dive in, immersing yourself in the sea and giving yourself to it, then you fully experience its magnificence.

Similarly, when you try to take from life and hoard a small bucket of it for yourself, whatever you get is not really worth having. It is when you dive in and give of yourself that you experience the real meaning and beauty of being alive.

Life is simply too grand and too magnificent for you ever to be able to take anything away from it. You can never take away and keep for yourself anything more than a mere token. When you really give is when you really live.

Leadership

The greatest leaders are those who lead not only with their words and ideas. The greatest leaders are those who lead primarily by their example. The most effective form of leadership is born out of the sincere desire and proven ability to make a positive contribution.

Those who lead best are those for whom leadership itself is not the primary aim. Those who lead best are those who can inspire others to embrace the positive values and priorities by which they themselves live.

True leadership comes not from position but from participation and effectiveness. Those who are willing and able to get things done are best suited to lead. To be a leader, be a shining example. Do that which you would lead others to do, and do it spectacularly. Leadership at its best enlarges and duplicates the efforts of the leader. Make those efforts the best they can be, and they'll result in true, effective leadership.

Three steps to success

The three most important steps to achieving anything are the last step, the first step and the next step.

The last step is the final step you take to reach the goal you seek. This is the step which clearly and precisely defines what you wish to accomplish. It's also an important step in charting a clear and specific plan of action. To develop a realistic plan for reaching your goal, begin with the last step. Next, determine the step before that, and then work backwards until you've constructed a solid connection between where you are now and where you wish to be.

The first step is also very important. Once you determine what it is, it's critical that you take that step right away. There's no point in setting a goal if you don't immediately start working toward it. No matter what the goal, there is always some step you can take right now. It is vital that you do just that.

The next step is perhaps the most important. From the time you begin until the goal is achieved, there is always a next step waiting to be taken. Keep taking that next step, step after step, and you will surely reach the goal.

It only works both ways

Part of providing value to others is making sure you receive value in return. For example, if you have a conversation with someone, and you do all the talking, neither one of you benefits as much as if there had been a give-and-take interaction.

Imagine what would happen if one of the major automobile manufacturers decided to give away its products for free. Initially, a lot of happy people would get free cars. Eventually, though, the company would run out of money. All the employees would leave. Suppliers would stop shipping parts. The company would no longer be able to produce any automobiles. In the end, the consumer would lose and the company would lose.

Lopsided transfers of value are never sustainable. It is in the best interest of everyone when value flows in both directions. Honor others by exchanging value with them. Don't cheat people by letting them take value from you without getting them to provide value to you in return. Don't spread the lie that there's such a thing by pretending to offer a free lunch.

Provide true, substantial, sustainable value to others by making sure you get value in return.

The price is the reward

For some reason, we like to think that something outside ourselves will cause us to be successful. We too often fall prey to fantasies of being lucky, or being in the right place at the right time, or getting in on a "ground floor" opportunity.

Those things happen, to be sure. Yet they are unreliable at best. The reality is that we really don't need to be lucky. While the chances of being in the right place at the right time are very slim, success is almost guaranteed for anyone who will do whatever it takes to achieve it.

Your success must come from you. What is success, anyway? It is the ability to live your life in the way that you choose, with purpose and meaning. No one can live your life but you. Success is not defined by the physical possessions to which you have legal title. It is defined by the way you live your life.

The only person who can make you successful is you. Sure, you might be able to acquire the tokens and appearances of success without putting yourself into it. But you will not have success. Success demands daily, moment-by-moment commitment and effort. Success requires that you put forth the best you have to give.

When success is achieved, it's interesting that those things which were previously considered the price of success — hard work, effort, discipline, persistence — also emerge as the key rewards of that very same success.

Give what you've got

Do you want to really feel great? Then give your encouragement to someone else. You'll find it impossible to be discouraged after putting so much energy into encouraging another.

Do you wish to be wealthy? Then find a way of adding wealth to the lives of others. Do you wish to be loved? Then give your love to another. Would you like to be more respected? Then show more respect for others.

Can a bright, shining light focus on itself? Of course not. Light has no meaning unless there is something to illuminate. In the same way, you have plenty of energy and overwhelming abundance, yet these only become evident, only become useful, when they're radiated outward.

Send your energy outward, where it will truly do some good. Shine your light on others and it will, in turn, make you glow. Life will reward you precisely to the extent that you express yourself, in your own unique way, to the world. Give what you've got and you'll get whatever you desire.

Start small

There are numerous billion-dollar companies doing business today which started only a few years ago with just one person — one person who had a big dream and who started small.

Anyone can start small and grow, whether it is in business, education, a relationship, or learning a new skill. Just because you start small, does not place any limit on how far you can go.

Starting small is infinitely better than never starting at all. If there's something ambitious you wish to accomplish, it's very likely that you won't get it all done in a single leap. But that is certainly no reason to give up on it.

Start small. There is something you can do right now to get it going. Then you'll be ready for the next step. Tomorrow, there will be something else you can add to the effort. Before long, you'll establish a powerful momentum.

In our world of e-mail, overnight shipping and microwave ovens, we too often think that instant gratification is the only kind of fulfillment that matters. But that is not the case.

Good things always take time. They always have and they always will, cyberspace notwithstanding. Do you have a dream? Have the courage and the patience to start small. Keep it up, day after day, and it will surely come to be as big as you want it to be.

What's in it for them?

The best way to gain the support and cooperation of others is to ask yourself this question: What's in it for them? A sincere and substantive answer to that question is better than money in the bank.

When you can offer real value, you'll have no problem getting real value in return. Remember, though, that real value is more than empty promises. Real value is more than hype, more than the mere appearance of value.

Avoid focusing too much on what you're offering or what you need. Instead, consider what they're getting. What can you do to truly make it more valuable?

Who stands to benefit more than you from the achievement of your goals, and why? Great fortunes are made by people who can answer that question.

A sad illusion

It has created untold strife for centuries. It has been the cause of hatred, anger, violence and countless wasted lives. It is the illusion that one person can profit from another's misfortune.

How can you possibly gain from hurting another? That other person is just as much a part of your world as you are. When you seek to hurt another, any appearance of a gain is far outweighed by the reality of the loss. If you seek to profit from the loss of another, it focuses you on the negative. That negativity, no matter where it is directed, becomes your own heavy burden. You cannot hurt another and avoid hurting yourself in the process.

Lasting fulfillment comes from being creative, not from being destructive. The creativity and positive energy you put forth come back to you many times over. So do the hurt and destruction. Which would you rather get back?

Pay the price

When you're ready to pay the price, only then can you truly enjoy and appreciate the benefits. If you get the reward without making the effort, it might look good, it might feel good, it might seem good. But it won't do you much good. It won't teach you or compel you to grow stronger as a person.

Have you ever played on a sports team that won a game by forfeit, because the other team did not show up? It's an empty victory. Sure, it goes in the win column, but it feels more like a defeat. After all, even though the goal is to win, the whole point is to play the game.

Is the point of life to collect trophies? The trophies have value only when they represent the effort you have made and the person you have become. Seeking to obtain the rewards of life without paying the price is like buying someone else's trophies at a garage sale. They may look impressive on your shelf but they bring no fulfillment and have no meaning.

Which would you rather have — the fruit or the tree? The fruit is gone after you eat it once. But the tree continues to provide fruit, season after season. The fruits of success are a poor substitute for actually living a life that brings success. Don't just grab the fruit and run. Take the time to plant and nurture the tree by paying the price and making the effort. Then you'll have all the fruit you could possibly need.

The bigger you

We each relate to the world from our own personal perspective. While that is valuable in many ways, it can also be limiting.

It is ultimately self-defeating to think that you can advance your own self interest at the expense of the bigger you — your family, your community, your world, the entire universe of which you are an integral part.

Everyone you know, everything you know, is connected to you in some way. Not by some mysterious cosmic force but by the simple, obvious fact that they are a part of your world, of your experience.

The quality of your life depends on much more than the state of your own personal body and surroundings. The quality of your life depends on the quality of your world. It depends on your willingness to take responsibility for that world. It depends on your ability to be a positive influence in that world.

Discipline

Steady and strong

The sun rises every morning. Though it is often a magnificent sight, it is nothing new. It has happened every day, over and over again, since long before anyone was around to observe it. The sunrise is not new or different. It is not "cutting edge" technology. Yet it is absolutely essential to life as we know it on this planet.

There is power in new discoveries, in fresh approaches. Yet there is enormous power in the steady, time-tested, "monotonous" pursuits as well. A magnificent new structure, utilizing the latest in construction technology, must still be built upon a solid, stable foundation held in place by the timeless ground.

Though it is vitally important to embrace change and progress, it is just as important to preserve and maintain a strong foundation from which to build. In your pursuit of what is new, be careful not to abandon that which is already working well. Those who are steady and strong, are in the best position to benefit from that which is new and exciting.

Go with time

If you want to move forward and grow more successful, ally yourself with something which always moves forward — time. Make time your friend and it will bring you great things.

It is futile to work against time by wishing that things had been different in the past. No matter how hard you wish, you cannot get time to reverse its sure and steady forward march. You're far better off if you turn around and march with it.

Time can leverage your efforts and give you the capability to accomplish things which otherwise seem beyond your reach. Do you want to write a book? Write a couple of paragraphs a day, and time will deliver your book. Do you want to build your business? Call a few prospects each day and time will provide a huge customer base. Do you want to speak a new language? Learn a couple of words each day and time will make you fluent.

Just about anything is within your reach when you use time to achieve it.

The middle ground

There's more to climbing a mountain than reaching the peak.

In between any desire and the fulfillment of that desire lies a vast middle ground of focused and consistent effort — much of it tedious, some of it painful, all of it necessary.

No matter how strong your desire, just knowing where you want to be will not get you there. You've got to cover that middle ground between where you are and where you're going. Before you can climb the mountain, you must first reach its base with the training, the resources and the energy necessary to make the climb. Then there's the climb itself.

Success comes from doing the dirty work, having the patience, making the cold calls, getting yourself prepared, being disciplined, staying committed, doing your homework, accepting responsibility, and continuing to take action.

Living the Wonder of It All

Winning comes not from crossing the finish line, but from running the whole race.

Discipline gets you there

Without self discipline, you'll run up against things you just cannot accomplish. You may be able to get by for a while on charm, intelligence, and raw desire. Yet sooner or later there will be something which simply cannot be done without discipline.

We tend to think of discipline in negative terms, at times using the word interchangeably with "punishment," as in "the student was disciplined for spray painting graffiti on the school property."

However, the only time discipline is negative is when it must be imposed on us by someone else. Self discipline, in contrast, is entirely positive and empowering. So you are left with a choice. You can neglect to exercise self-discipline and subject yourself to the discipline of others, which can often be harsh and painful. Or, you can discipline yourself and reap the many rewards.

Nothing better to do

The thought that there's something better to do will constantly nag at you and distract you if you let it. When you're thinking that there's something better to do, you begin to resent what you're currently doing. Your focus suffers. Your commitment suffers. Your effectiveness suffers.

Whatever you're doing, work as if there is nothing better to do. That way you can finish that work competently and effectively, and move on to whatever is next. Bring all your commitment and focus to the task at hand. If the "something better to do" thought comes up, quickly put it out of your mind by saying to yourself, "No, that's of no concern right now."

Of course you have priorities. Some things are certainly more important than others. Yet if you waste your time while doing the "little things" wishing you could be working on the "big things," how does that benefit you? Give your complete focus and attention to the little things when necessary, and you'll end up with more time to devote to the big things.

Details

Setting ambitious goals is a great start. Yet it is not enough. Real success comes only when those goals are followed through to their achievement. That means paying attention to the day-in, day-out, nitty-gritty details which go into making the goal a reality.

Anyone who thinks they're too important to be bothered by details will eventually be undermined by their own arrogance and ignorance. Details matter. Details are supremely important. Details are very much worth knowing about.

Certainly you want to delegate tasks and responsibility when appropriate. Certainly you want to keep your eye on the "big picture." But don't neglect the details.

Get the details right. Paying attention to details can make the difference between a losing team, and one that wins the championship. Details can give your business a sizable competitive advantage, or they can put you out of business, depending on whether you attend to them or not.

Dive into the details. Know them, respect their importance,

and they can make all the difference in the world for you.

More for your effort

Those who begin soonest end up getting the most accomplished from their efforts. If you want your work to really pay off, begin it right away. Waiting will only make the job more difficult and time consuming when you eventually get around to it.

Time exerts a powerful leverage, and you can use it to your advantage. The results of your efforts today will multiply and compound as time goes on. On the other hand, if you wait until the last minute, that leverage works against you. Hurrying to complete something at the last minute is terribly inefficient. There's so much more you can accomplish with the same amount of energy when you start earlier, rather than later.

When there is work to be done, get started right away. That's by far the easiest, most effective approach. Though it may seem at the moment that putting it off would be easier, you know from experience that's definitely not true.

Would you rather accomplish more or accomplish less? Get started right away and you will accomplish so very much more for the time and effort invested.

Remember the basics

Let's face it. Achievement is no picnic. It is hard work. It is often tedious. The most spectacular success is not easily or quickly won. To accomplish anything worthwhile frequently requires doing the same thing, over and over again and again, for as long as it takes. Winners focus on mastering the fundamentals, rather than chasing every new gimmick that comes along.

You've probably seen this happen many times in your own town. A trendy restaurant will promote an exciting new "concept", draw crowds for a few months, and then lose most of its business to the next new fad. Meanwhile, other restaurants focus on perfecting their food, their service, their dependability, their cleanliness, their convenience and their reputation — and build a loyal clientele which stays with them for the long haul.

Sometimes we become so familiar with the fundamentals, that we forget how important they are. Yet no one is so accomplished, or so highly experienced, that they can afford to ignore the basics.

Often the most exciting and significant results come from the most tedious efforts. Remember the basics. Persist and you will prevail.

Free yourself

The more you avoid doing what needs to be done, the more burdensome you make each moment. Those things you've put off until later can build up and drag you down with regret, worry and negativity.

Putting something off until later is certainly no way to free yourself from it. Instead, such procrastination and avoidance actually extends and expands whatever it is you desire to avoid.

One of the most liberating things you can do is to free yourself from the gnawing burden of a task you've been avoiding.

And the way to achieve such freedom is simply by going ahead and doing what needs to be done.

Rather than continuing to worry about it, rather than putting your energy into making excuses and rationalizations, just go ahead and do whatever you've been putting off. The sooner you get it done, the better off you'll be.

Just think how great you're going to feel when it's done. Imagine how great it will be to free your energy, your mind and your spirit from the burden of procrastination that has been hounding you.

Don't worry for another minute about something you've been putting off. Go ahead, make the effort, and enjoy the immense freedom and satisfaction of already having it done.

Temptation

It is tempting to think that you can have something for nothing. It is tempting to think that you can take shortcuts. It is tempting to think that you can avoid the negative consequences of your destructive behavior.

When we're tempted to do what we know we should not, it is a deception. We see the reward, obsess over it, and mentally build it up bigger than life, completely out of proportion to reality. At the same time we fail to see the significantly bigger downside.

Being positive does not mean ignoring the negative consequences of our actions. Living positively comes from avoiding the negative consequences by refraining from the destructive behavior which surely leads to them.

The next time you are tempted to act against your own good judgment, remember that it is a lie, a deception for which you will ultimately and unavoidably suffer. Be positive by clearly seeing the negative and staying away from it.

Success is tedious

Success is often tedious. When we see success in others, it looks exciting and fun. We see someone who is successful in business living in a magnificent house, driving a shiny new car and taking exotic vacations. We see a successful athlete being cheered by the crowd after a winning performance on the playing field. We usually see only the results of success in others.

What we often fail to see and appreciate is how they got there. The person with a successful business has spent many long, boring hours, working late into the night on tasks that no one would consider fun or exciting. The winning athlete has spent day after day on the practice field and in the weight room, laboriously training mind and body.

Those who understand, appreciate and accept that the road to achievement can often be tiresome, those who are willing to do whatever it takes, no matter if it is often tedious and boring, are the ones who will get the reward they seek.

The long view

The magnitude of your success and fulfillment will be in direct proportion to how far ahead you consider the consequences of your actions.

If you have no thought or consideration for your consequences beyond the present moment, you'll be successful on a very small scale, chasing from one immediate gratification to another. As you begin to extend the consideration of your consequences further and further into the future, your level of true success will grow.

Every action has consequences, not only now but far into the future. For a particular action, the immediate consequences may be desirable, and yet the future consequences of the same action may be disastrous. To enjoy the most success, take the actions which have the most positive consequences over the longest amount of time.

Smoking a pack of cigarettes may be somewhat pleasurable today, but it can have very negative consequences on all the subsequent days. Investing a thousand dollars in a mutual fund might be a bit of a sacrifice today, but it can continue to have very positive consequences for a long time to come.

Success consists of thinking ahead, of considering future consequences, and of taking actions based on those considerations. Make the overall, long-term consequences positive and enjoy the benefits long into the future.

The joy of discipline

How do you think of discipline? Most of us know and understand the value of disciplined, focused effort, yet we find it difficult to put into practice. Thinking that we need to be more disciplined is one thing — actually being more disciplined is something else altogether.

And it is in the thinking about discipline that we often set ourselves up to falter. We think of discipline as doing without. In order to focus on one thing, we see ourselves giving up all the other things we could be doing at the moment.

Yet discipline is ultimately enabling, not restraining. Without discipline, we have possibilities. With discipline, those possibilities become reality. Rather than giving up anything, discipline allows us to choose which of our many possibilities we most want to express.

Discipline is so much more practicable when you see the reality of what you're doing, rather than lamenting the fantasy of what could have been. Disciplined effort brings you what you want. What could possibly top that?

The wind will blow

If you go outside on a cold day and forget to wear a coat, the wind will have no mercy on you. You can complain and protest all day long that you had every intention of wearing a coat. You can offer dozens of sound and reasonable excuses for why you didn't wear a coat. Still, the icy wind will continue to chill you to the bone. When you go out in the cold without a coat you suffer the consequences.

Should you expect any other endeavor to be different? If you want to stay warm, you remember to wear a coat. If you wish to be believed, you always tell the truth. If you desire to accomplish anything, you discipline yourself to take the necessary action. If you'd like to be wealthy, you find a way to create value.

Complaints, excuses, maneuvering, anger, despair and petulance will change none of that. There is an immutable connection between actions and their consequences. Attempt to break or shortcut the connection, and your efforts will be in vain. Yet to the extent that you respect and employ the connection, life will bend to your every wish.

Living With Persistence

Persist

With enough persistence, tiny, soft droplets of water can wear away the hardest stone. With persistence, a small seed can grow into a towering tree. With persistence, anyone can make a difference.

With persistence, one small effort builds on top of the one before, until the combined force is undeniable. Small, focused efforts, strung together over time with persistence and determination, bring about magnificent results.

So much effort is wasted because it is spent against itself. In our impatience we zigzag off in so many different directions, and end up covering very little ground. Only by focused persistence we can reliably and consistently make progress, and utilize our efforts for all they're worth.

Where do you want to go? Who do you want to be? What do you want to accomplish? What possibilities are waiting for you to fulfill? Persist, and you will.

Determination

Think of a time when you were truly determined. Think of a time when you were willing to do whatever had to be done, in order to get the results you had decided upon.

Visualize that time, put yourself back in that circumstance, and feel, once again, the driving power of your own determination. Experience, once again, the confidence which comes with being so determined that nothing can stop you.

Now imagine what that same level of determination could do for you today. Imagine what would happen if you applied the power of determination to your current situation.

Think of all the obstacles and difficulties you could move on past. Think of all the positive, valuable goals you could reach.

Being determined, and staying determined, is hard work. And yet it is powerful, productive work that gets you where you want to go.

You know how powerful and energizing your determination can feel, and you know the valuable results it can bring. So call it up, put it to use, and take yourself with determination to those places where you truly want to go.

One more effort

When you feel like giving up, it's a very good sign that you're truly making progress. So by all means keep going.

Eventually you're going to reach the point where just one more attempt, one more effort will bring real success. What a shame it would be to give up just as you reached that point.

You do not know what the next effort will bring because the future is not based on the past. That feeling of wanting to give up is based solely on the past, which really doesn't matter any more. What matters now is where you're headed, not where you've been. And when you view it from that perspective, giving up is simply not an option.

Living the Wonder of It All

Success is always achieved after one last effort. You're working your way toward that point, and you may very well already be there, ready to make that very effort.

So keep going, keep making the effort, no matter what has happened before. Somewhere up ahead is that one more effort, the one that will take you all the way to where you want to be.

Weakness into strength

It doesn't matter that you've stumbled a dozen times, or a hundred, or a thousand. You can still get up and move forward just as surely and quickly as if you had never fallen.

Today is a brand new day, and the very place where you are is a starting point from which anything is possible. Get on with the business of living to the fullest. Never before have you had as much experience, or as much desire to move forward, as you do this very moment. Now is your time to really get it right; now is your time to shine.

Every weakness you've ever known can be a source of strength the moment you decide to overcome it. As soon as you see what has been holding you back, you've identified a powerful way in which to move forward.

It doesn't matter what your limitations have been or what they continue to be. What matters is your resolve to move on past them. For as soon as you know what to do and why to do it, it has already begun to happen.

Get back up

You cannot prevent every setback. However, you can make it a priority to recover quickly from them and get back on track. In every effort there will be interruptions, disappointments, even some disasters.

Your recovery time depends largely on what you decide to make it. The time and energy you put into anger and self pity will serve mainly to prolong the time it takes to get going again.

Accept that the setbacks will come and when they do, decide to move quickly past them. Find something positive in each one, and that will serve to get you focused again on progressing toward your goal.

Winners and losers both stumble. The winners are the ones who quickly get back up and keep on going.

The moment of truth

You've persevered through the dark, difficult times. You've taken each challenge in stride and overcome countless obstacles along the way. And just when you're beginning to turn the corner, just when it looks like it's all starting to go your way, a huge setback comes along and knocks you down. Just when things are starting to go well after a long and difficult effort, the momentum is suddenly snatched away from you.

That is when it is most important to not give up, to keep on going. Pick yourself up, no matter how discouraged you may be. Now is your opportunity to cross the threshold into a realm where success is virtually assured.

You were so close and then the world beat you back yet again. Find a way to keep on going. It is indeed a moment of truth. When you can pick yourself back up, weary though you may be, and get back in the game, at that moment you'll know

116

with absolute certainty that nothing can stop you, that nothing can keep you down.

What would you attempt if you knew you could not be stopped? Keep going, no matter what, and you'll reach truly magnificent heights in whatever you choose to undertake.

Make it big

Start small. It is where everyone starts. It is where every achievement starts — as a small, fragile thought. Anyone can start small. That is the beauty of true success. It doesn't have to be grand or magnificent in the beginning; in fact it cannot be.

Start small and then keep going. Keep growing, learning and adding to your achievements. Success is attained not by those who start big, but by those who maintain their momentum long enough to get big. Every day counts. Every moment counts. You can allow them to work against you, or you can make them work for you.

Where do you want to go? What small thing can you do right now to get you started? The most stunning achievements you could possibly imagine each began with a small thought, an idea, a desire to make a difference. What is your thought, your idea, your desire? Follow it and keep nurturing it until it is real. It may be small now, but you can make it big.

Do what you can

Do what you can, when you can, where you are, with whatever you have available to you. Though you may not have enough time or resources right now to finish, you have some time available to get started.

Every book that was ever written, no matter how lengthy, was written one word at a time. Every race that was ever won was completed one step at a time. Great accomplishments come from stringing one effort on top of another.

With enough small efforts, anything can be achieved. Though you may not have the time or the resources to make a big impact, use what you do have to make a small difference. Do it often enough, with commitment and focus, and the big results will surely come.

Don't waste the time you have by complaining that there's not enough of it. Use it to do what you can. As quickly as time is used it is replaced, but if you don't use what you have right now, you'll never get the opportunity again.

Do what you can, every opportunity you get. You'll soon find yourself getting exactly where you wish to go.

The momentum of success

Every great achievement builds on accomplishments that preceded it. The new, powerful computers which we now use were designed and produced using the previous generation of computers. New works of literature are full of allusions to earlier works. Artists develop techniques which draw heavily from previous methods. Successful businesses often adopt and improve upon the strategies used by others.

Whatever you wish to accomplish, you don't have to start from scratch. Rather than begrudge the success of others, find a way to build upon it. With each achievement there are countless opportunities for even greater achievements. As the world grows more successful, there are more and more ways to become successful.

The same concept applies on a personal level. Even a very small success, can be used to build a greater success. Achievement has infinite potential. Anyone can start with a small accomplishment. And when you do, you're on your way to greatness.

Persistent or stubborn?

Sometimes in an attempt to be persistent, we become stubborn. That's a mistake, because there's a big difference between the two. Persistence is the ability to keep your eye on the goal, to continue plowing ahead despite the challenges, to doggedly work your way past any obstacle. Yet persistence also demands flexibility. Stubbornness, on the other hand, is a refusal to accept reality and an unwillingness to adapt to changing conditions.

To reach any goal requires that we be unyielding about where we intend to go, while at the same time flexible about how to get there. Unfortunately, many times we get it backwards — we persistently do the same thing every day, out of a sense of habit or comfort or lack of knowing what else to do, even if it is not taking us in the direction we want to go.

Few things ever come to pass in exactly the way that we plan them. The ability to adapt is very much a part of relentless persistence. When you're persistent about what you intend to accomplish, and flexible as to how it will happen, anything is possible.

Time to succeed

Give yourself time to succeed. Patience and persistence make almost anything possible. The only way you can fail to reach your goal, is to stop before you get there.

If you're not there yet, keep going. What a waste it would be to stop now. Starting over will take even longer. Keep going. Success is just a single step away from failure. Get yourself to the point where you can take that final, single step and then you're there.

Time will come and it will go, no matter what you do. Time will bring you to your goals, if you choose to make the most of it. Take the time to succeed. Make it work for you. Persist. You're on your way. Keep going and you'll get there.

Long road ahead

Just because the road ahead is long, is no reason to slow down. Just because there is much work to be done, is no reason to get discouraged. It is a reason to get started, to grow, to find new ways, to reach within yourself and discover strength, commitment, determination, discipline.

The road ahead is long, and difficult, and filled with opportunity at every turn. Start what needs starting. Finish what needs finishing. Get on the road. Stay on the road. Get on with the work.

Right now you're at the beginning of the journey. What a great place to be! Just imagine all the things you'll learn, all the people you'll meet, all the experiences you'll have. Be thankful that the road is long and challenging, because that is where you'll find the best that life has to offer.

Work on it anyway

At first your dream will seem impossible. Work on it anyway, and it goes from being impossible to improbable. There's now a tiny glimmer of hope. Still, even though it is possible, even

Living the Wonder of It All

though it could happen, most likely it won't. Work on it anyway.

Keep working on it, and soon you'll realize that it probably will happen. Your efforts have elevated your dream from impossible, all the way to likely. You start to feel that you've got it made, yet now is not the time to stop. Work on it anyway.

Then, the bottom drops out. Life throws you an unexpected curve. It all falls apart. Suddenly, your dream is not going to happen. Work on it anyway. Look for a way to make it happen. You've come too far to give up without a fight.

Work on it anyway, and you'll find a way to reclaim your dream. The obstacles which seemed so insurmountable, were actually just the final step on the road to fulfillment of your dream. You've finally arrived — you've attained your dream and life is great. Work on it anyway. Now is your chance to reach even higher.

Get Beyond Being Stuck

Do you feel like you're stuck where you are, unable to move forward? Does it seem that when you take two steps ahead you then fall back three? Are you trying desperately to get ahead and yet falling more and more behind? Do you know precisely what you want to accomplish, and how to do it, and yet you just cannot bring yourself to take the necessary actions for a long enough period of time?

Do you keep trying to live positively, to give of yourself, to make a real difference, and the world keeps throwing it back in your face? Does it seem that you're completely overwhelmed?

That feeling of being stuck is actually a very positive sign. It means that you're truly ready to begin moving yourself forward. To illustrate, let's look at an example. Imagine that you drive home from work on Friday afternoon, park your car in the garage, and accidentally leave on the car's interior light without knowing it. You go in the house, enjoy a lovely dinner, watch a film on television, and go to bed. All the while, the light has been draining your car's battery and at about 3:00 am, the battery runs completely out of power. But of course you don't even realize it. On Saturday morning you get up, have breakfast, take a walk and then spend most of the day working in your garden. The weather is beautiful and you're having a wonderful time. Later in the afternoon you get cleaned up and ready to go meet some friends for dinner.

You then walk out to the garage, get in the car, turn the key in the ignition switch, and nothing happens. Your battery is dead and your car won't start. You are stuck. But you didn't realize you were stuck, you didn't feel stuck, until you were ready to go somewhere. All that time you were walking through the neighborhood and working in the garden, you didn't feel stuck. It's only when you really are attempting to get somewhere, and are somehow prevented from doing it, that you truly feel stuck.

So that feeling of being stuck means that you are indeed ready to move forward. It means that there's somewhere you really want to go, even if that somewhere is "anywhere but here."

So what's the next step? Let's go back to the car battery story. If the battery is dead, what needs to happen? You need to get a jump start. A pair of jumper cables connected to another vehicle's battery will get you up and running in no time. But let's think for a moment about the things that will NOT get you up and running.

Being angry at yourself for leaving the light on will not get you going. You can fill yourself with rage and resentment for leaving that light on, and still when you turn the key nothing is going to happen. When you're feeling stuck in your life, it can be easy to become angry with yourself. After all, you're the person who is most responsible for getting you where you are. Though it's useful and positive to accept that responsibility, it is of no use to be angry or resentful about it. What's happened has happened. The best you can do is to learn from it. Holding on to the anger will only delay your moving forward. So accept responsibility for where you are, and then also accept the reality of where you are, without fighting against it but rather with a desire to truly do something positive about it.

Being angry at the car manufacturer for making the light so easy to leave on will not get you going. You can rant and rave about how poorly designed the car is, and yet when you turn the key nothing is going to happen. You're still going to be stuck. When you're feeling stuck, it is very easy to blame others for your situation. In many cases, other people are indeed very much to blame. Yet the process of assigning blame is not going to move you forward. Sure, it can make you feel better to know that your troubles are not entirely your own fault, but you'll still be stuck. In order to get beyond being stuck, you must put your focus elsewhere.

Feeling sorry for yourself, and receiving the sympathy of others, will not get you going. If your car battery is dead, you can call your sister who lives two hundred miles away and she can make you feel better by being very sympathetic over the phone, but there's nothing she can do to get your car going. She can encourage you to do something about it, and that encouragement can be extremely useful, yet you're still going to need to go beyond merely being encouraged and to actually do something about it.

Thinking of excuses will not get the car going. Certainly there are things that stand in your way. The car is pulled into the garage and will be difficult to reach with jumper cables. You don't know anyone who has jumper cables. You're all dressed for dinner and don't want to get your good clothes dirty. Those are all very valid facts. Yet to get yourself going you must view them as obstacles to be overcome rather than as excuses for not taking action. When your life seems to be stuck, it's easy to see all the things standing in your way. One by one, these are things that must be overcome if you are to move forward. Viewed together, they may indeed appear to be insurmountable. But you don't have to conquer them all at once. You're not going to get past them all in an instant. It will take a con-

Living the Wonder of It All

tinuing effort. You're fully capable of working your way through one obstacle after another, until you eventually make your way through them all.

Positive thinking alone is not going to get the car going. Yes, it's great to have a positive outlook on life. Yet that positive outlook, that positive thinking, is only the beginning. In order for it to make a difference, you must act upon it. It's great to have a lot of positive ideas and plans for moving forward. To actually move forward, you must act on those plans, you must put those ideas into motion. Let positive thinking guide your actions, and let your actions make those positive thoughts a reality.

We've taken a look at some of the things that will not get you going. So what exactly will get you moving ahead, past the point of being stuck?

One of the most reliable ways to get beyond being stuck is to start small. To illustrate this, let's look at another example. A week or two ago, I was doing some repair work and needed to replace a 3/16 inch diameter steel cable. I had purchased a 12-foot piece of this cable but I needed to cut it down to about 10 feet long. The problem was, I didn't have a tool capable of cutting the cable. So I took the "divide and conquer" approach. A 3/16 inch steel cable is actually made up of many, much smaller wires wound together. I did have a wire cutter capable of cutting the smaller wires. So I used a pair of pliers to untwist the strands, and then used my wire cutter to cut each individual one. It took some time but eventually the entire cable was cut to the length I needed.

Over the years, problems and challenging situations can build up and twist together like the wires of a steel cable to the point where they are holding you firmly in place. When you tug against the cable itself, you go nowhere. You simply do not have the strength to break free of it. Yet if you look closely at that cable, you'll realize that it's made up of small, vulnerable strands — strands that you can begin to break, one by one. So start cutting those wires. Go to work on the obstacles one by one. It will take some time, yet during that time not only will you be cutting yourself free, but you'll also be building your confidence with each small victory. And before long, you'll be moving rapidly ahead.

Another way to move past being stuck is to keep your focus on where you're going rather than on the fact that you're stuck. Constantly repeating to yourself and others that you're stuck is going to reinforce that fact in your mind, and affect all of your actions. So even while you're still stuck, start acting like you're not.

For example, let's say you feel stuck in a certain part of town and would like to be able to move to a new neighborhood. Rather than being miserable about where you live, start to actually enjoy the place where you would like to live. Drive over there on a regular basis, park your car, and take a walk through the neighborhood where you want to move. Do your shopping over there. Eat in restaurants or attend a church or join a sports club in the neighborhood. Find a way to start living and acting as if you were past the point of being stuck where you are. And while you're doing it, realize that you are, in fact, doing it. You're moving solidly and substantially past the point of being stuck. You're not wishing and hoping and dreaming about being there, you're actually doing something to get yourself there.

In order to move past being stuck, you need a lot of energy. There's plenty of energy available to you, but much of it is probably being drained away. If you live in a cluttered, messy environment, that drains and distracts you. When you straighten it up and become better organized, it frees up a significant amount of energy which you can use to move forward. Or perhaps you're being drained by knowing that there's someone you need to forgive, or by something important that you've been putting off until later. Maybe you're eating too much junk food and not getting enough exercise. Or there could be people in your life who constantly drain your energy away. To get past being stuck, look for those negative situations that drain your energy and start eliminating them or getting away from them.

Often when you're stuck, it's because you're being held back by assumptions that are no longer true, or assumptions that may never have been true at all. These assumptions can take the form of "I could never" such as "I could never sell anything" or "I could never learn to use that computer program" or "I could never find the time to exercise." Assumptions such as these, when repeated often enough, firmly become a part of your reality. They become so thoroughly ingrained in your thinking that you forget they're there, yet they very much continue to exert their influence. Your assumptions are so much a part of you that they can be difficult to examine and even more difficult to change. One useful approach is to step back and look at yourself as if you were someone else. Look at what you think and what you do as if you were an independent observer. Consider how you would view your thoughts, actions and assumptions if your brother, or your cousin, or your neighbor were making them instead of you. It's extremely likely that you have some assumptions which are simply not true, and which are keeping you stuck where you are. By making the effort to uncover those assumptions, and then discarding them, you free yourself to move forward.

Finally, to get past being stuck you must give yourself permission to move ahead. That sounds a little strange, but the fact is that no matter how unpleasant being stuck might be, it is still, in some ways, very comfortable. It's what you know, and moving away from being stuck means moving into unknown territory. Much of what keeps you stuck is your own reluctance to move away from the comfort of what is familiar, even though what is familiar may be quite painful. So give yourself permission to do it. When you hear yourself start to make excuses, tell yourself, "It's OK. I know it's uncomfortable and challenging, and I know I could think of lots of reasons to stay right where I am, yet this time I'm truly committed to moving myself forward. I give myself permission to ignore the excuses, no matter how compelling they may be. I give myself permission to persist in accomplishing what I have decided to accomplish and what I truly want to do."

No person, no thing, no circumstance can keep you stuck where you are when you are committed to moving ahead. If you're stuck, there are plenty of things you can do right now, and plenty of things you can continue to do, that will get you to where you want to be. Others can give you lots of help and encouragement, yet ultimately it is something you will do for yourself. When you feel stuck, you've already taken the first step. You've experienced the reality that there's somewhere else you want to go. That desire itself is compelling evidence that you do indeed have the means to get there. So act on it. Let go of the anger and frustration, resist the temptation to feel sorry for yourself or to seek the sympathy of others, move away from those things that are draining you, and start working your way through the obstacles, one by one. Cast off your negative, outdated assumptions and give yourself permission to move past the point of being stuck, and into new and exciting territory.

Living the Wonder of It All

Living With the Best of Expectations

Who is holding you back?

What if someone were to actively prevent you from achieving success? What if there was a person who sabotaged your efforts at every turn? How would you feel about that person? What if that person was constantly coming up with reasons to discourage you, always talking you out of taking action?

What if that person was you? It very well may be.

Quite possibly, you are your own worst enemy, when it comes to pursuing success and achievement. Do you ever catch yourself saying "I could never do that"? Does that little voice inside you express disdain for your goals, and come up with dozens of reasons why they can't be achieved?

The limitations placed on you require your cooperation if they're to hold you back. The good news is, you don't have to cooperate. That little voice inside your head can say anything you want it to say.

Do you really want to be the primary advocate for your own limitations? Of course not! Just imagine what you could accomplish if you were one hundred percent supportive of yourself. Now, stop imagining and start living it. Your limitations are powerless without your cooperation, so choose to leave them behind in the dust as you reach for the stars.

Go for the best

It is nearly impossible to remain discouraged for long when your goal is compelling enough. If you're discouraged, the answer is not to scale back your dreams, but rather to expand them to the point where you cannot help but be pushed forward by them.

The challenges, the obstacles, the difficulties are going to be there, no matter where you're headed. So you might as well be headed toward where you truly want to go. You won't always be able to control which challenges come your way, yet you can control what rewards are on the other side of those challenges. Make those goals, those dreams so big and so meaningful that the challenges will seem trivial by comparison.

Your expectations will determine your attitude, and your attitude will determine your actions. Your actions, in turn, will determine the results you achieve.

Your future is yours to create, regardless of what has happened in the past. Imagine the best, expect the best and you'll know that you have what it takes to get there.

Free your expectations

What do you expect of yourself? What do you expect of others? In most cases, what you get is very close to what you expect. You'll rarely earn more than you expect to earn. And you'll rarely earn less. Other people will usually deal with you the way you expect them to.

To improve your results, first improve your expectations. When you truly expect to earn more money, you naturally find a way to do so. When you respect others enough to expect the best of them, they'll come through with a stellar performance.

Base your expectations not on what has happened in the past. Rather, let your expectations be guided by what you desire for the future. Set your expectations free of the artificial limits imposed by previous disappointments. You have every reason to expect the very best for the future. When you do, you will most certainly find a way to make it happen.

The seed

We are full of energy and in need of direction. When that energy is guided toward creative achievement, the results can be spectacular. Plant the seed of encouragement in the fertile ground of a person's life, and it will grow into magnificent accomplishments.

Anyone has the capacity to do great things, yet far too few know it or believe it. No matter how fertile the ground may be, if no seed is planted, nothing will grow. How many lives have been wasted in misery and destruction because they never received even the smallest seed of positive encouragement?

A seed is tiny. Yet when it is planted in the right place and at the right time, and nurtured with care, that tiny seed can grow into a ceaselessly abundant harvest.

Think of the lives around you where the seed of encouragement can take root and grow. Think of the difference you can make when you encourage yourself and when you offer your encouragement to others. Think of the seeds that you have the opportunity to plant. Spread the seeds of encouragement far and wide, and delight in the bountiful harvest that they will surely bring.

Yes

How many opportunities have you lost because you could not, or would not, say yes to them? Certainly it is important to say "no" when appropriate. Otherwise you end up making commitments that you cannot possibly keep. Yet it's also vital that you be able and willing to say "yes."

The good things we seek rarely come to us in exactly the way we have imagined. If we're constantly saying "no" in order to avoid even the slightest discomfort or inconvenience, we soon find ourselves missing out on the richness of life, wondering why our dreams never materialize.

Saying "yes" takes courage and faith. Really meaning it, takes effort and commitment. Saying "yes" gets you involved. True, it forces you out of your comfort zone, but what do you really want — comfort or fulfillment?

Great things are always coming your way. Make sure you say "yes" to the best of them.

What do you expect?

Have you ever done something foolish and then asked yourself afterward, "why did I do that?" It's a good question. In fact its such a good question that it deserves to be pondered before taking action.

We're tempted to do so many things out of habit, out of spite, or out of anger. More often than not, we come to regret the things we do and the words we say under such circumstances.

Yet it doesn't have to be that way. It's really very simple to act, speak and live with intention. Just ask yourself, before taking action, what you expect to accomplish. Think of the pain that could be avoided by that simple question. Consider how much wasted effort could be redirected toward accomplishing something of value, just by acting with a little bit of forethought.

What do you expect to accomplish with what you're doing? There's no point in taking action, if it doesn't get you anywhere. So think before you do. It only takes a moment, yet it can bring a lifetime of valuable rewards.

You know it

You know you can do it. You know you can achieve it. You know you can. Think of yourself accomplishing the goal which you want more than anything else. Think of how your life will be when you've done it.

Your sincere desire for anything is proof that you know you can do it. If you didn't know, at some level, that you could do it, how could you even conceive of it? Yes, there are doubts but they are on the surface and are quickly left behind as soon as you start to take action.

Your desire makes sense only because you know you can. Would your spirit waste its precious time compelling you toward something that was impossible for you? Of course not. You can do it. You know you can.

In the strength of your desire is the confidence you'll need to make your dreams a reality. Because you know you must, you also know you can. And because you know you can, you must. Otherwise, the regret would be painful indeed. You can do it. And you will. Make the effort. Without a doubt, you know you can.

Make it happen

What is one thing you've always wanted but you never thought you'd be able to do, or to be, or to accomplish? Just for a moment, drop all your doubts and consider that it is indeed possible.

It may not happen in exactly the way you envision it. Yet there is some way, some means by which the essence of your desire can and will be fulfilled.

Fulfilling your most treasured desires — the ones you truly desire, not the ones the world tells you to pursue — is not about selfishly getting what you want. It is about becoming the best you can be.

Just thinking for a moment that something could be possible is enough to raise your level of positive energy. You can feel it even now. That positive, empowering feeling is the first important step in truly making it happen. Your most sincere desire points the way to your most meaningful purpose. Listen to it, feel it, know it is possible, and you'll begin right now to make it so.

What's your mission today?

It is easy to spot people who are on a compelling mission. They're noticeably determined, focused, energetic, enthusiastic and unstoppable. The excitement surrounding their goal is infectious and they easily enlist the support of others. No obstacle is too great, but rather is another challenge to be overcome.

In reality, everyone is always on a mission. It's just that most "missions" are not all that exciting, and too many people jump from one to another. Yet at any point in time, we're all committed to something.

What is your mission for today? Is it just to get through the day with the least amount of effort? Or is it something so exciting, so compelling that people are lining up to join you? Whatever you're fully committed to, will happen. Make the commitment to live out the exciting possibilities available to you, today and every day. Make your mission worthy of the wonderful person that you are.

Proceed

What would you do right now if you knew that everything today would turn out perfectly? What project would you start, what person would you talk to, what problem would you tackle if you could be assured of success?

Is there anything you're putting off because you're afraid of failure? Is there anyone you're avoiding because you're afraid of what they would say or think?

There is no guarantee of success. But there is a guarantee that if you never go for it, you'll never have it. And even in the failed attempts, you'll learn and grow. There is no guarantee that other people will think highly of all you say and do. But that's their problem.

Do you believe in the worth of your own pursuits? If so, then what could possibly prevent you from following them? If you're looking for a sure thing, then here's one — everything you achieve will come only from the things you attempt. In order to succeed, you must proceed. Today is a great day to start.

Expectations

It is easy to change your expectations. You can do it in an instant. And that can be a problem. Too often, we lower our expectations because that is easier than overcoming the obstacles which stand in the way of fulfilling those expectations.

Are you being forced to lower your expectations, or are you simply choosing the easy way out? You must expect the best in order to achieve the best, yet it takes more than just expectation. It takes effort and commitment. If you lower your expectations at the first sign of difficulty, it seriously erodes their value.

Don't lower your expectations to meet your performance. Raise your level of performance to meet your expectations. Expect the best of yourself, and then do what is necessary to make it a reality.

The odds of success

If you desire to achieve success, the odds are against you. Outstanding success is so celebrated and admired precisely because it is so exceptional and difficult to achieve.

In terms of sheer numbers, the odds are against you. But the odds don't matter. Because success does not result from blind chance. There really are no odds, as such. There are only results.

You have every opportunity to make your own results. Your results are not determined by statistical percentages. They are determined by your own action and commitment. The fact that only a small number of people in your position ever make it to the top, has nothing to do with the opportunities available to you. In fact, the more the odds are against you, the more special it makes your achievement.

Put the odds in your favor by refusing to let them limit your possibilities.

Can you do it?

Do you really think you can do it? Sure, you have a goal. The clearer and more specific it is, the better. But when you honestly evaluate your goal in your heart of hearts, when you look at it as realistically and objectively as you possibly can, do you really think you can do it? Or in the end, is it just wishful thinking?

The way to make it real, the way to truly know without a doubt that you can do it, is to know and understand exactly HOW you will do it. What specific steps will you take to bring you from where you are right now, to where you want to be?

You can accomplish whatever you decide to accomplish. That takes action. Before you can do it, you must know what actions to take. Have you thought about that in detail? What exactly is your plan? When you know precisely what to do, you'll know with complete confidence that you can do it. There is a way for you to do it. Determine what that is, see how you yourself can do it, and you'll have the belief to carry you through.

Living in Control

Remote control

What if there was someone, sincerely acting in your best interest, who had a remote control device that guided all your actions? Similar to the remote control for a television or VCR, the device could switch between different "channels" of activity, and increase or decrease the "volume" of energy which you put forth.

Just imagine how effective you could be if, at just the right time, the button was pushed for "focused, disciplined work" or "creative problem solving" or "aerobic exercise" or "compassion" or "gratitude." If someone who really knew what they were doing could control your actions, there would be no limit to what you could achieve.

In fact, there is someone who can do that. That someone is you. And the guidance you give to every single one of your thoughts and your actions, is much more powerful and compelling than any "remote control" could ever be. Your control over your own life is so much a part of you that you probably don't even think about it. Yet it is there. You are under your complete control, and with that you can do countless great things.

Take responsibility

Those who would convince you to abandon responsibility are, without exception, intending to take advantage of you. When you give up responsibility you give up power over your own life. When you abandon your own responsibility you open yourself up to being cheated and betrayed. Those who offer to "relieve" you of responsibility do not have your best interests at heart, even though they may act, or pretend to act, out of a sense of compassion.

There is no way around the fact that to have more power and influence over your own life you must take responsibility for it. The more fully you maintain responsibility for your life, the more influence you have over your own circumstances. It is a formula which can lift you up or cut you down, depending on how you respond to it.

Though responsibility is an effort, it is also a profound joy. Imagine admiring some great achievement and knowing that you are largely responsible for making it happen. That sense of accomplishment has no equal. The more responsibility you take for your own life on a moment by moment basis, the richer that life will be.

Make it yours

Don't wait for someone to give you permission to succeed and achieve. Get yourself busy and do it. Don't wait for someone to tell you how to do it. Take it upon yourself to figure it out. Don't wait for just the right situation. Don't count on being lucky. Do what it takes to make your own good fortune.

Learn from others. Seek the advice, input and feedback of those whose opinions you respect. But don't depend on anyone or anything to do it for you. Make the best of fortunate situations, but don't depend on luck or chance.

Depend on those things over which you have the most direct

control — your own thoughts and actions, your ability to make the choices which will lead to precisely where you have decided to go.

Your destiny is in your hands. Think like it and act like it with each passing moment. Take hold of that destiny and make it the best it can possibly be.

Your response

You cannot stop the sun from rising or even hold it back for a fraction of a second. Yet you can control where you'll be and what you'll be doing at the instant that it makes its appearance. Often you have no control over the many things that come your way. Yet you always have control over what you do about them.

Today, things will happen that you did not plan for, that you did not cause, that you did not anticipate. You can fight against them, building up a wall of resentment and frustration that will stop you cold, or you can adjust to them and continue on your way.

Long ago you learned to adjust to the time of the sunrise each day, to the movement of this massive planet as it spins through space. Certainly you have the ability to deal with all the other things outside your control, both great and small, which will come your way.

For everything that can bring you down, there's a positive response that will lift you up above it. The challenge of successful living is to find that empowering response. And steadily follow it toward where you want to be.

Resent, or resolve?

Resentment will only make a bad situation worse. Resentment mainly serves to prolong and empower whatever it is you resent, and that's certainly not what you want.

So rather than being held down by resentment, use the same energy in a much more positive way. Simply decide to turn your resentment into resolve.

Instead of staying focused on what's wrong and who's to blame, put that same energy into changing it for the better. The more difficult and painful the situation, the more reason you have to move beyond it, and the more resolve you can develop for doing so.

The same factors which lead to resentment can just as easily and just as powerfully lead to resolve. Any time and every time you have the urge to tie yourself down with resentment, you also have the choice to move your world forward with resolve. When given such a choice, choose resolve. It will take you to much better places than you ever could hope to reach with resentment.

Little choices, big results

If presented with the choice, would you choose to be healthy, wealthy, secure in your relationships, happy and fulfilled, or would you choose a life filled with illness, poverty and despair? That's an easy decision. Anyone would choose the first alternative without even thinking about it.

In fact, you do have that choice. It isn't usually presented to you in such a momentous way, and it never comes as a single choice. Rather, the quality and direction of your life depend upon the many, many choices you make, moment after moment, day after day, which build on one another to fashion the reality of your world.

The little choices you make, the ones that seem not to matter much, soon add up to produce big results. They directly affect the life you live. Over the course of every day, you're presented with an overwhelming number of choices. As you make these choices, keep yourself clearly focused on where you want your life to go. Make the appropriate choices, one by one, day after day, and you will be headed powerfully in the direction of your own choosing.

Your control

Some people, upon encountering things which are beyond their control, throw up their hands in despair and frustration. Others understand that by using those things which they can control, it is possible to turn any circumstance in their favor.

Long ago people realized that they had no control over the seasons. Some of those people, however, also realized that by controlling their own actions and movements in accordance with the progression of the seasons, they could have plenty of food to eat. Great civilizations resulted which continue to grow and thrive even to this day.

In every area of endeavor there are numerous and significant factors beyond your control. Yet you are far from helpless. In every situation, there are countless positive actions you can take which will more than make up for the things you're unable to control.

Life is yours to live. Excellence is yours to pursue. Focus not on what is beyond your control. Instead, exercise control over your own thoughts and actions so as to harvest a sweet fulfillment from the vagaries of life.

It's your energy

When was the last time anxiety knocked at your front door? Have you ever met stress walking down the street? When did you ever answer the telephone and discover anger on the other end of the line?

Things such as stress, anxiety and anger do not exist in real, tangible form. They exist only in you and only with your co-operation. They are not grown in a field or manufactured in a factory. They are created in your head.

And as such, there is no need for you to "deal" with them or "resolve" them. You have it in your power to simply annihilate them or, better yet, to avoid giving birth to them in the first place.

Do not let your anxieties control you. Do not let them do anything. Do not let them be. Just throw them away. What good are they? Why allow them to clutter and complicate your life? It takes a lot of energy to create and to maintain stress, anxiety and fear. Redirect that energy toward something positive and creative. It's your energy. It's your life. Use it to be joyful.

One a day

Challenge yourself today to change just one thought from negative to positive. As you go through the day, be aware of your negative thoughts and select just one to turn around.

Is there someone of whom you've always held a negative opinion? Now's your chance to change that. Is there something you've always thought you could not do? Perhaps you'd like to reconsider. Find just one of those negative thoughts. Then find a way to make it positive.

You are in control of your thoughts. Those negative, limiting thoughts which "come to you" are in reality coming from you. You have the power to change them. And when you do, great things can happen.

So give it a shot. Discover how readily you can change your thoughts, and how effective that can be. Just imagine what your world would look like if you changed only one negative thought each day. Think of the new perspectives you could gain, and of the opportunities that could open up for you.

Take the challenge today. Pay attention to your negative thoughts. Select just one and make it positive. Discover what an immediate and valuable difference it can make in your life and in your world.

What does the future hold?

The future holds nothing. And it has room for everything. No crystal ball can accurately bring it into focus because there are just too many possibilities. Certainly you can get an idea of what is likely in the future. But the best thing about your future is that it's up to you.

You are the most important participant in your future. All the micro-fads and mega-trends pale in comparison to the influence that you have right now on your own future.

What does success mean to you? How do you wish to live your

life? What kind of a future would you like to see? Today you have an opportunity to answer those questions. More importantly, you have an opportunity to fashion those answers into reality.

The future is open, ready and waiting for your influence. Choose your future, and thrill to the challenge of making it happen.

Victim or victor?

Have you chosen to be a victim or a victor?

Victims say "I'm too busy." Victors say "I'll find the time." Victims look for excuses not to even make an attempt. Victors look for ways to get it done. Victims ask for pity. Victors look for challenge.

Victims worry about who is to blame. Victors find a way to make a difference. Victims complain. Victors take action. Victims find comfort in the weakness of others. Victors help others to develop their strengths.

Victims agonize over yesterday's losses. Victors prepare for the opportunities of tomorrow. Victims take credit. Victors accept responsibility. Victims search for quick and easy answers to their problems. Victors spend the time and effort needed to build the life they desire.

In each day are abundant opportunities for you to be a victim, and just as many ways for you to be a victor. The choice is yours. How do you wish to live today?

Rise above it

Often, the people you encounter can be petty and unreasonable to the point that life becomes very frustrating. Seek to rise above it. Refuse to let it get to you. Honor your commitments, do as you said you would, be polite, be helpful, and don't allow yourself to get drawn into someone else's small-mindedness.

If you react with anger or spite, then they have succeeded in pulling you into their petty world. Instead, respond with all the integrity you can muster. Be confident — but not arrogant — that what you are doing is the right thing. Be confident enough to set the agenda. Have the strength to not let the little, small-minded things get to you. Your time and your life are more valuable than that.

Defend yourself, yes. But without being defensive. Claim the high ground. Take the initiative to focus on substance instead of triviality, on possibilities instead of condemnation. Think like a winner. Act like a winner. Rise above the squabbling and put your energy to use making a real difference.

Accountable

Life holds us accountable whether we like it or not. Every action produces irrefutable consequences. And though we may try to hide from those consequences, in the end they always catch up to us.

What will you do today to uphold the responsibility you have to your own possibilities? What about in the next twenty minutes? What consequences will your actions produce?

Hold yourself accountable, and the consequences work in your favor. Accept the responsibility for your own life, and you gain control of your own destiny. It's easy, and often very reasonable, to blame your troubles on something or someone outside yourself. It's easy to expect other people, or changing conditions, to solve your problems for you. It's easy to expect dumb luck to bring fulfillment into your life. It's easy, and yet sadly misguided.

Ultimately, only you can be accountable for you. It is a serious responsibility and a boundless opportunity.

Making the Most of All You Have

What you have

Sit beneath a magnificent oak tree, and realize that everything the tree has ever needed, has come to it. The nourishing food, minerals, water and sunlight, all have been flowing past the tree, or within its reach, for the entire life of the tree. Though by its growth it has reached out, not once has the tree had to go anywhere to get what it needed.

The tree grows and prospers by its ability to make use of what's available, right where it is. The strong, towering, enduring tree has accomplished its impressive growth by simply using what it has.

The next time you feel you have to go somewhere, or get something or struggle in some way, in order to be happy, or in order to accomplish something, think of the mighty oak tree.

It is wonderful that you can move about, and that you can cause so much to happen. Yet in all your doing and going and getting, don't neglect what you already have. Richness and fulfillment come not from simply getting more, but from making full use of what you have.

You have it in you

Within you there is courage. Within you is determination.

Within you are focus, discipline, and strength. Within you are the qualities and abilities that can bring you anything you want to have, and take you anywhere you wish to go, and make you the person you choose to be.

These strengths and abilities are within you, waiting to be called upon. They're ready for you to use them. They're available to you at a moment's notice.

All you must do is decide to use them. And that will happen when you find a clear enough, strong enough reason. Perhaps you've already glimpsed that reason. Perhaps you're already on your way.

The strength you need is yours. The courage, the discipline, the determination are already a part of you. When you are truly ready, they'll be there.

Make the most

Make the most of your mistakes by admitting them and learning from them. Make the most of your opportunities by being prepared to take advantage of them. Make the most of your disappointments by letting them strengthen you.

Make the most of your relationships by acting with gratitude, respect and consideration. Make the most of your time by keeping in mind how precious each moment is. Make the most of your frustration by accepting its energy and turning it toward positive pursuits.

Make the most of your work by constantly looking for ways to provide more value. Make the most of your weaknesses by letting them guide you toward improvement.

Make the most of tomorrow by making a difference today. Make the most of your life by living each day with joy, passion and purpose.

The possibility is there

In a tiny seed is the possibility for an entire forest. If that possibility is to become reality, the seed must be planted in fertile ground. Then it must be nurtured and nourished, day after day.

Your greatest possibilities are much the same. They can become grand and glorious achievements, or they can become nothing at all. It depends completely on the care and nourishment they receive.

Just as a seed needs sunlight, water, nutrients and a firm ground, your possibilities require time, effort, commitment, belief, focus and discipline on a daily basis, so that they may grow to their full potential. Great achievements cannot be built from feeble materials. To fulfill your possibilities requires the best you can be. Every day is important. Every moment makes a difference.

With each thought you think, each action you take, each moment you live, you have the opportunity to either nourish your possibilities, or feed your regrets. Right now is no exception. A grand achievement depends on what you do with this very day.

Serious threat

If your life were suddenly threatened, would you take action to protect it? Of course you would. Your life is extremely important and you would do whatever possible to avoid losing it.

For most of us, the biggest threat to life is not sudden or dramatic; it is inconspicuous and incremental. By far, the most common threat to life is that we waste so much of it on trivial and meaningless pursuits. Those things steal life away just as surely as a murderer or a fatal disease.

As you go through each moment of this day, keep in mind how very precious and important these moments are to you, because they are what make up your life. Each one can bring great richness and fulfillment. It would indeed be a shame to waste them on useless and petty pursuits.

Right now you have an opportunity that is unequaled by anything you can possibly imagine — the opportunity to be alive and effective. It is a great and wonderful thing that is too often taken for granted. See your life for the truly special, valuable opportunity that it is, and make the most of every single moment.

Use this moment

Waiting for the perfect time will never bring it about. The sooner you get started, the more you'll get accomplished. Is there something you've been putting off? Why let another valuable day go by? Begin right now to make it happen. There is always something you can do. There is a first step that you can take right now. Take that step, and then take the next step. Work steadily and consistently toward the goal.

Circumstances will never be ideal, but that doesn't really matter. You can achieve whatever you desire no matter what the circumstances may be. Your actions and your level of commitment have far more influence than mere circumstances.

The choice you have is this. You can wait for the world to

change, or you can be the one to change it. Indeed, the world will change no matter what you do. Yet the more influence you have on that change, the better you'll like the results.

Excuses are available to you in abundance, but of what value are they? Forget the excuses. Forget about waiting for the perfect moment. Now is the time to get started. Use this moment and each following moment wisely, and you'll get precisely where you wish to go.

Live your value

There is an abundance of value hidden inside of you, more than you could possibly imagine. Yet as long as you continue to follow the same old routine, seeing the same people every day, sitting in front of the TV, never venturing out of your comfort zone, that value will remain hidden and unreachable.

The way to uncover your hidden value is to put yourself on the line, to get involved in life. Attempt something challenging, meet new people, stretch your limits, see new places, and subject yourself to new experiences. Challenge and intensity will uncover in you skills, talents, abilities and interests you never knew you had.

You are full of wonderful possibilities. Do something with them. The most painful regrets, those which never go away, are regrets for things not done, things never attempted.

Every day is an opportunity to live, to really live and experience. Grab that opportunity today, and make the most of it. Live the abundance that you already have. Claim the richness of life that is yours even now. Be the passionate, fully alive person you were born to be. Live your unique value and delight in the wonder and beauty of it all.

Excellence

Excellence is not a skill. It is an attitude. Excellence comes not from education, money, ability or connections alone. It comes from a commitment to do the very best with whatever you have available.

Excellence is very valuable, and it is open to anyone who commits to follow it. Excellence is always in demand, in any field of endeavor, in any economic climate, in any set of circumstances.

Excellence comes from thoroughness, from attending to the necessary details while staying clearly focused on the purpose. Excellence comes from a sincere desire to make a positive difference.

No matter what the task, if it is followed through with excellence people will take notice. The effort you put into creating excellence will be effort wisely invested. Everyone has the opportunity to produce excellence in their own way, and it is an opportunity that anyone would do well to capitalize on.

Your priceless time

Money can be saved for later. And money that is wasted can be earned back. But time must be used as it comes, for once a moment is past it will never come again.

You have exactly one chance to make the best of today. And that opportunity is upon you right now. The time you spend today can bring a magnificent and lasting return, or it can bring a lifetime of regret.

Today can never be replaced. It is yours to use right now. You cannot save it for later, but you can turn it into an achievement that will continue to bring value long into the future. Time can be priceless or it can be worthless, depending on what you do with it.

This very day is a vein of the purest gold, waiting to be mined. Your efforts will make that treasure a reality.

On your side

Put time on your side by making use of every moment. Put truth on your side by being truthful. Put respect on your side by genuinely offering it to others. Put honor on your side by living honorably.

Put momentum on your side by acting with persistence. Put opinion on your side by being thoughtful. Put wisdom on your side by learning from each experience. Put hope on your side by finding the positive in every situation.

Your strongest advantages are the ones which come from the way you live your life. Your most effective efforts are the ones which come from your heart. What you truly value will bring true value to you.

Having enough

The more you depend on things outside yourself the more frustrated and miserable you will become. Take responsibility for your own fulfillment, for your own joy, for your own happiness. These things need not be conditional, or dependent on factors outside your control. Stop waiting for permission to be happy. Give yourself permission and start living each moment with joy.

Living the Wonder of It All

"If only I could find a new job and make more money, then I would be happy." Do you attempt to console yourself with false assumptions such as this? By all means, make every effort to put yourself in a great job, but don't fool yourself into thinking that it will bring you fulfillment, or that the lack of it will prevent you from being happy.

You will be fulfilled and happy when you realize that you already have enough. And that depends entirely on you. Accept and live out the abundance that is already yours, and nothing in the world can hold you back.

Use it now

Today will proceed right along, no matter what you do. You can't stop it, and you can't hold on to it. What you can do, is use it for all it's worth.

You can choose to put forth the absolute minimum effort necessary to make it through this day, and you will indeed make it through the day. Trouble is, tomorrow you'll end up right back where you started, with the need to make it through another day.

Instead, use today for all it's worth. Make the effort to make some real progress. You know what needs to be done. You know what you want to accomplish. Now is the time to do it.

Instead of "making it through" focus on "making it happen." Think of one little thing you can do today, that will improve all your tomorrows, and then do it. Surely you have the time and energy for one little improvement. Think of the difference it will make.

When you're already moving sideways, it doesn't take that

much more effort to change your direction to forward. Today is here right now. Use it!

Something will grow

Something will grow in the garden of your life today. Will it be an unsightly weed or a beautiful flower? Will it be what you've planned and created by your thoughts and actions, or will it simply be what you've allowed by your carelessness and lack of clear direction.

Whatever you plant will grow in the fertile ground that is today. Fail to plant, fail to tend the garden, and something will still grow there. But it probably won't be to your liking.

Walking through a neighborhood, it is easy to spot the gardens which are carefully and lovingly tended. They're the bright and bountiful ones. Likewise, a life that's well tended is filled with the bright, beautiful rewards of that care and effort.

What will grow in your life today? The fertile ground is waiting for the seed of your purpose and the care of your commitment. Today you can grow something of value and beauty. Just decide to make it so right now.

Living the Wonder of It All

Living Fully
in the Moment

Right Now

Stop for a moment and calm your thoughts.
Let go of your anxieties and look around you.
What do you see?
You see a world filled with beauty.
You see a life filled with possibilities.
You see dreams being born,
being nurtured and being fulfilled.
Yes, there are challenges.
Yes, there is sorrow.
Yes, there is violence and hatred.
But more than these there is love,
there is goodness, there is joy.
The future is uncertain.
And that means there's
no limit as to how
beautiful and joyful you
can make it.
Yet what you have is right now.
And right now is completely as it should be.
It is your time to live.
Think of what a precious thing your life is
and how truly blessed you are to be experiencing it.
Right now.
Right now, any anxiety you may have about the future
is only an illusion.

Let it go.
Let it fade away as the beauty and perfection of
right now wash over you.
The best thing you can do for the future
is to live with everything you have in the present.
Right now, you are in a position to create real,
lasting positive value for the world in which you live.
How do you do that?
By following your heart.
By being the you that is really you.
You may have wandered away from yourself.
Now is the time to come home.
You know in your heart that you're here for a reason.
The pain you feel is that purpose, that reason for living,
as it constantly aches to break free.
When it does, you'll be more alive than you ever
could have imagined.
Breathe in the beauty around you,
the beauty and richness of being alive.
It is your gift.
It is your fortune.
It is your blessing.
And it is yours, to live, to experience, to fulfill.
Right now.

Paradise

Are you living in paradise, and you don't even know it? Are the ripe, juicy fruits of joy and fulfillment yours for the picking, while you continue to dig for sour berries? Are you walking down streets littered with sparkling diamonds, and not even bothering to look at them, much less pick them up?

Do you pass by golden opportunities every day, during the few moments you spend outside the secure, comfortable prison cell that you've built for your life? Are the boundaries

Living the Wonder of It All

which separate you from true fulfillment, of your own making?

In each moment there is gold, waiting to be mined. In each friendship there is joy, waiting to be felt. In each problem there is wealth, waiting to be created. Open your eyes. Open your heart. Look around you, really look, and see the beautiful world where you could be living, if only you would.

Magic in every moment

Electrons dance in front of your eyes and you call it color. Waves of air sweep over you and you call it music. The massive sphere on which you dwell rotates a few degrees and you call it sunset. There is magic in every moment. Behind even the most mundane occurrence is an entire universe of abundant wonder.

If you could sense every detail of something as simple as the falling of a raindrop, it would completely overwhelm you. And yet raindrops fall all the time.

In every action, no matter how seemingly insignificant, there is a whole universe of power. In every moment there are infinite ways in which to make a very real difference. You are always streaming full speed through an abundance of options and possibilities.

See the possibilities. Feel the power. Make your own special magic today.

Small pleasures

Be happy with the little things, because there are so many more of them. Don't postpone your enjoyment of life until after some grand achievement. Strive for that grand achievement, to be sure. And take pleasure in all the joys along the way.

Every day presents you with countless opportunities to experience happiness. There is joy available in each moment, if you really want to find it.

Consider how very much more likely you are to persevere, and to reach that grand achievement, if the path to it is filled with delight. Find enjoyment in the small things, and even in the striving. It will keep you going. Relish the journey, and it will help you reach the destination.

Beautiful life

The beauty you see around you is already inside you. If it were not, then it would not appear as beauty. As you delight in a magnificent vista, or an elegantly created work of art, remember that the beauty you admire is always yours. Its power is within you regardless of possession or physical presence.

In this sense, the beauty in the world is mainly a reminder of the incredible beauty that is your life. It is great to have those reminders which renew and fulfill your sense of beauty and appreciation for it. Yet the essence of beauty is not in the objects which you call beautiful, it is in the wonder and magnificence of life itself.

The power of beauty is a living power, and it is yours to apply. The beauty you sense around you is merely a hint of the abundance of beauty that is your life. Yes, there are challenges. Yes, there are tragedies. Yes, there is pain. Still, through it all, every moment of every day, you have the beauty and richness that is your life. Feel the awesome power of that, and live it.

Living the Wonder of It All

Happiness is here

Happiness is far too valuable to be put off until later, or buried in the past. Happiness is here for you to bring to life in the only place where you can truly experience it, the present moment.

Being happy right now will not make your problems any worse. In fact, it will most likely make things better. Your happiness will not harm or offend anyone else. In fact, it may very well be of much value to others.

Happiness has no prerequisites, no conditions which must first be met, really no requirements at all. Experiencing happiness does not in any way deplete it, but increases the supply of it.

Stop waiting for happiness to come to you and start letting it come from you. And there will always be more than enough to go around.

Get past the past

Your shortcomings and disappointments are all in the past now. They have nothing to do with what you can accomplish from this point forward. Every day, you start with a clean slate. Every moment is an opportunity to begin the process of turning your dreams into reality.

It doesn't matter what has happened before. Yes, the past has brought you to where you are. Yet right now the path splits off in an infinite number of directions. And you have the choice of which one to take.

Learn from the past and then let it go. To wish that it had

been different, is a waste of time and energy. To continue living with your past limitations, is a waste of your life's enormous potential.

Your past does not define who you are or what you can accomplish. You do.

Just enjoy

Give yourself the powerful, refreshing and energizing gift of pure enjoyment. Take a moment, or several moments, or even longer if you wish, and let yourself just enjoy.

Look, really look, at the world around you and see the beauty in every direction. Listen to the harmony and rhythm of life's sounds. Feel the warmth of bright sunshine, the coolness of running water, the rush of a breeze on your skin. Take a long, deep relaxing breath of fresh air.

Explore and experience the overwhelming beauty and wonder of the reality which extends in every direction. Let go of any expectations, judgments or analyses, and allow yourself to peacefully experience it all as it comes to you.

We often get so caught up in planning, organizing, adjusting and responding that we end up with no time to simply experience and enjoy. Yet the moments spent in pure enjoyment, free of guilt, anxiety or expectations, can be truly valuable in a way nothing else can be.

On a regular basis, give yourself a refreshing mini-vacation. Take some time to just enjoy. Put your world and your life into perspective and reap the rich rewards of being able to truly enjoy who you are, where you are, and what you're doing.

Some days

Some days you become weary. Really rest for a while, not too long, then get back on track with renewed vigor and purpose. Some days you become satisfied. Be careful not to let that stop you; build enthusiastically on what you have accomplished. The greatest value is of no value if it is not put to use.

Some days you'll be sad. Take comfort in knowing that your sadness is possible only because joy is also possible. It is painful and yet it is beautiful that you're able to care so much. You'll get through it.

Some days will be frustrating. Though you have the best of intentions, though you make a genuine effort, the results fall short of the mark. Learn from these days. Take a deep breath. Know you're making progress even if it doesn't seem so.

Some days will be joyful. Treasure these days. Live them completely and with no remorse. They are yours to live and to hold as well. Fully experience them so that they will be with you always.

Along the way

You can get things done without enjoying yourself. You can also enjoy yourself without getting anything done. However, the best approach is to get things done while also enjoying yourself. That's the way to reach long term success, building one accomplishment on top of another.

If you aim to simply enjoy yourself without getting anything done, then the result is — you don't get anything done. You may be very positive and cheerful, at least for the moment, but after a while it will seem quite empty. On the other hand, if you're driven to achieve, without any consideration for the quality of your life along the way, that can be empty, too. Sure, you'll get what you want. But you're also likely to get burned out and resentful.

Make the effort, move toward your goals, and delight in the moments along the way. When you enjoy the journey there's never any reason to stop.

Live the joy

Imagine nothingness. Imagine being surrounded by absolute nothingness. There is no light, no sound, no sensation, no form, no hot, no cold. It is difficult to even know if you are alive or not.

As you float through this nothingness, suddenly you feel your feet hit something solid. You look around, and there is light, there is a beautiful blue sky. A cool breeze gently blows against your face and leaves rustle in the trees above your head. Suddenly you are in a world full of color, sound, and sensation. Many others like you are there, too. You can move about, you can communicate, you can create, you can drink in the beauty, and explore to your heart's delight. This wondrous place is not without its challenges. Yet the incredible possibilities open to you make the problems seem trivial by comparison.

This is not a fantasy. You are really here, right now. You've had the good fortune to land on this magnificent shore, where each day holds a new treasure. Now, live the joy.

Stop holding back

What would you do if someone else treated you the way you treat yourself? How would you react if someone criticized you the way you criticize yourself? How would it be if someone forced you into the same self-defeating behavior that you choose to do on your own? What if someone else prevented you from enjoying life as much as you deny enjoyment to yourself?

You would, no doubt, be outraged. You would probably file a lawsuit, or have them arrested, or seek revenge. And yet each day you hold yourself back, and hardly even notice.

If you would never let someone else treat you that way, why do you allow yourself to do so? You have control over your own actions, your own thoughts, your own feelings. Stop defeating yourself. Allow yourself to live, permit yourself to succeed, let yourself enjoy life.

Be good to yourself. You deserve it.

Be beautiful

Nothing stirs the spirit in quite the same way as beauty. There is something inside of us which resonates with productive, joyful energy in the presence of beauty.

Beauty is difficult to define, yet easy to recognize. It can exist on a grand scale, and in the smallest detail. Beauty is a mountain peak, the smiling eyes of a child, the intricate workings of a powerful machine, a musical passage, elegantly designed software, a convincing idea. Beauty compels and inspires like nothing else.

What do you do that's beautiful? You don't have to be a painter or a poet to create beauty. You don't have to be a supermodel to be beautiful. Anything undertaken with passion and commitment can produce beauty. The greatest, most celebrated achievements are always beautiful in their own unique way.

Be the best that you can be. In your work, your play, your world, your life, be beautiful.

A special day

Our lives are full of special days — holidays, birthdays, weddings, anniversaries, days of celebration, days of remembrance, fellowship, and leisure. We treasure those special days when we take time to celebrate and enjoy life, when we get together with loved ones, when we give a little more of ourselves and find special pleasure in the simple joy of being alive.

And the most special day of all is... today! Because today is where we live. Today is full of possibility, ready and waiting to be filled with life and love. Today brings the opportunities and challenges which give meaning to life. In every moment of today, there is treasure.

Every day is special because we make it special. No matter what the calendar says, each and every day is full of opportunities for life, for love, for making dreams come true. The weeks, the months and the years come and go. Along the way we collect fond memories of the past and build hope for the future. Yet today is when we do our living, when we create the memories and fulfill the hopes.

Life is full of special days — one right after the other. All the special days in the past have brought us here today. And all the special days to come, begin to take shape right now. Today is indeed a special day, a sacred gift that is ours to fulfill.

Living Peacefully

Peace

Peace is not something that happens to you, nor is it the absence of anything happening to you. Peace comes from who and what you are, and how you choose to be. The world around you can be full of turmoil and strife, and yet you can be at peace in your own heart.

Peace is one of the surest signs of strength. Those who lack confidence feel the need to lash out. Those who are strong have what it takes to stay calm. When your identity and fulfillment are tied to fleeting, superficial things it is impossible to remain at peace. When you invest your being in true and lasting values, and when you remain ever vigilant to those values, you develop the confidence and strength to be peaceful.

Peace cannot be forced on anyone, and true peace cannot be forcibly taken from anyone. Peace comes to those who are strong enough and wise enough to choose it, and with that peace comes an abundance of living which is otherwise impossible to know. Choose peace, and by the strength of your choice, help it to grow.

A few steps away

Take a few steps away from the chatter and confusion to a place where you can see more clearly. Take a few steps away and give yourself a new and empowering perspective.

You'll see that much of what concerns you, need not concern you. You'll see that the problems are more than overwhelmed by all the opportunities and positive possibilities.

You'll see that many of the things which hold you back do so only with your consent. You'll see how easy it can be to let them go and to let yourself move forward.

Take a few steps away, to a place where you can focus on what is truly important. It's a place where your purpose really matters, where your efforts truly and easily make a positive difference.

Life is beautiful, and filled with an unending stream of wonderful possibilities. Take a few steps away from the noise and confusion, and you'll see the best of those possibilities come clearly into focus.

Peaceful, focused effort

Though there may be a thousand things demanding your attention, you can only really devote yourself to one at a time. If you're to make any headway at all, in your work, your relationships, your life, you must focus your efforts.

One of the best ways to achieve focus, is to pursue and maintain a calm, peaceful approach to life. Tell the noisy distractions in your head to be quiet. For a moment, put everything out of your mind. Think of nothing. Stop your thoughts before they start. Enjoy the serenity of just being. Then, selectively, put back into your mind only that on which you wish to focus. Keep yourself free of all the rest.

Living the Wonder of It All

Take pleasure in the satisfaction that comes from peaceful, focused effort. Enjoy the level of accomplishment that you can achieve when all your energy is flowing in the same direction. Calm down, stay focused, and you'll be much more effective at getting it all done.

Cool it

Actions taken in anger are at best ineffective. Anything done in anger will almost surely lead to regret. Most things done in anger are blind and unthinking reactions, rather than controlled and intentional responses. When you let your anger take over your actions, you put yourself at a distinct disadvantage.

The best thing to do when gripped by anger is to wait. Count to ten. Count to 100. Sleep on it. Think it through. Talk it over. Get past the anger of the moment before you take the next step. Certainly anger can provide energy, but it is almost always a reckless and uncontrolled energy which harms anything in its proximity, including you.

Acting in anger hurts you at least as much as anyone else. Wait out your anger. The energy does not go away. Instead, it becomes more focused and productive. Whatever caused your anger, there's something positive you can do about it. When you take time to let the anger cool, you'll find that positive course. Be smart. Cool off and be a real winner.

Peaceful moments

Sometimes the best way to move forward is to slow down. Bigger, busier and faster are not always better, though we often assume they are without even thinking about it. A full calendar does not necessarily mean a full life.

You work hard for your life. Spend some significant time living it. You make many sacrifices for your family. Spend some real sustained and joyful time being with that family, free of schedules or expectations. Live the richness that you so often strive to attain.

Stop and enjoy the things you normally hurry past. Spend some quiet, calm, peaceful time, not as an item on your schedule, but apart from it. Let down your defenses, let go of your expectations, give up your pretenses and simply enjoy the supreme beauty of being alive.

Calm your thoughts

Have you ever noticed how much your own thinking can often interfere with your awareness? You've probably had the experience of failing to hear what someone is saying to you because you're busy thinking of how to answer them.

There is a time for thinking, for questioning and judgment, for analyzing and strategizing, and there is a time for opening yourself up to experience the world around you. You are well equipped to think, and you are also equipped to listen, to feel, to see, to experience.

Thoughts can be powerful. The absence of thoughts can be powerful as well. Many things are annoying, for example, simply because you think they're annoying. What grand and beautiful things might lie hidden underneath the relentless noise of your own thoughts?

Pursue your thoughts with vigor, and when the situation calls for it, let your thoughts be still. Strength and wisdom come not only from excitement and complexity, but also from a quiet and peaceful awareness of what is.

A peaceful mind

Great ideas and great accomplishments flow easily and naturally from a calm and peaceful mind. When you are free to think and act in the direction of your most treasured dreams and highest vision, there is no limit to what you can accomplish.

But when your mind is filled with resentment or regret, it cannot do its work. When worries are bouncing around inside your head, they crowd out the valuable and useful thoughts. When anger clogs your thinking, your mind has trouble getting anything done. When envy infects your thoughts, it's difficult to focus on anything else.

So put your mind at ease, free your thoughts, and let them move you quickly forward. Experience how wonderful and refreshing it can be to release your mind from the burden of negativity.

No one is forcing you to hang on to your anger, so let it go. Nothing can make you worry unless you choose to worry. Whatever is possible, is possible for you, so there's never any reason to be envious of anyone. Let all those negative thoughts simply fall away from you.

You are blessed with a powerful and effective mind. Keep it calm, keep it peaceful, and fill it with the thoughts that will move you quickly ahead.

Peaceful power

Your world cannot be at peace until you yourself are at peace. Calm your worries and fears. Let go of your anger and resentment. Look at each difficulty as an opportunity to strengthen your ability to remain peaceful.

When your mind and your spirit are at peace, your thoughts and actions are free to be strong, focused and effective. You cannot force others to be truly peaceful. You cannot shame them into it. Yet by your example you can draw them into the power of your own peacefulness.

Peace will not come to you until there is peace that comes from you. Living in peace does not mean giving in or giving up. Rather, it means having the confidence to let go of your anxieties and insecurities, so you can focus on your positive possibilities.

Decide to live this moment, this day, this life in peace. And though the world around you may swirl with turmoil, you'll be moving positively forward with others sure to follow.

Calm and confident

You cannot extend a deadline by worrying and fretting over it. You cannot make a difficult decision by agonizing over it. You cannot get anything productive accomplished with anxiety.

Calm down. Relax. There's a job to be done and you might as well be your best. Your efforts are largely wasted when they're undertaken with stress and apprehension.

Stop fighting against your circumstances. Stop worrying about the unfairness of it all. Success and fulfillment are not beholden to circumstance or luck. You attitude and your actions are what make the difference. And they can be whatever you choose.

There are plenty of excuses to be stressed out, but there's no good reason to be. Stress and anxiety only serve to hold you back that much more.

Relax. Take a deep breath. Be calm, be happy and let yourself move forward with confidence. Your efforts will flow freely and effectively when you stop attempting to force them.

Enjoy peace

Live today in peace. Peacefully accept what is, and work diligently to make of it what you wish. Act with peace toward others and you will be enjoy more peace yourself. Have the courage and strength to spend some time in silence and contemplation.

Let go of fear and guilt. Replace them with kindness and forgiveness. Rather than fretting over what is most impressive or most strategic, put your energy into doing what is right. Use your judgment not as a weapon for putting down others, but as a tool for building your own character.

Look past the things that usually annoy you. Marvel at the beauty of the world in which you live. Stop rushing so frantically. It accomplishes nothing. Make your efforts measured and determined. The results will be undeniably magnificent.

Decide to live this day in peace. See how powerful that can be. In peace there is strength. In peace there is effectiveness, purpose and determination. Experience the power of peace today and understand how very rich life can be.

Living Through the Challenges

The ultimate challenge

Imagine that you're the wealthiest person in the world, with a vast and powerful fortune at your command. You can have anything you desire. There is no luxury or pleasure that is beyond your reach. You have no need to work for a living. Your fortune is large enough to last for thousands of lifetimes.

All this is great for a few years, but after a while you discover that there's something you desperately want, something you desire with everything that's in you, something with which you are completely obsessed day and night. And it is something you cannot have, despite all your riches and power. It is the challenge of creating something from nothing.

Then you realize that there is a way to have what you desire. You desperately want it, so you give away most of your riches, give up the majority of your power, and become the person that you really are right now, living exactly the life that you're living right now.

Finally, you have what you want — challenge. You are filled with excitement, anticipation and even a little fear — and for the first time you feel truly alive. You've given up everything you ever had to get to this exciting place. Now, how will you make the most it?

Energized by challenge

Do you want to truly energize your life? Would you like to bring razor-sharp focus to your thoughts and efforts? Then set a challenge for yourself.

Make it a real, substantial challenge — something with personal meaning and something that will truly stretch your limits. A compelling challenge will bring out the very best that you're capable of giving. Challenge will boost your energy level and focus your attention like nothing else can.

You are designed and equipped for responding to challenges. Throughout history we've seen that peak performance levels go hand-in-hand with the most difficult challenges. Challenge strengthens. Challenge motivates. Challenge compels, and even demands.

Challenge will take you beyond where you thought you could go. It will expand your horizons and introduce you to exciting new possibilities. It will bring a richness to your life that no amount of money or comfort can equal. Seek challenge and you'll find the best of yourself.

Gravity

Every person on this planet is constantly under the influence of a powerful limiting force called gravity. Gravity makes difficult the lifting and movement of massive objects. It makes our feet tired and actually causes us to become shorter as we age.

Although gravity is a powerful limitation, we would not want to be without it. As fun as it might appear to fly in space and frolic free of gravity, the absence of gravitational force yields its own set of very difficult problems. With no gravity, you'd have to tie down all of your furniture, food crumbs would migrate to every corner of your house, your computer's mouse would wander off, and you'd never be able to fill your bathtub for a warm, relaxing soak. Gravity, as limiting as it is, also makes many things possible, including the very existence and stability of the planet.

So it is with every limitation we face. We can never hope to be free of limitations, nor would we want to be. Many of the things which appear to limit us in some ways, actually support us in other ways. Every great thing that has ever been accomplished, has been done by people with limitations. Rather than wishing for a life free of limitations, let your limitations give you strength.

Freedom

Freedom comes not from living without a care, nor does freedom come from the absence of difficulty and challenge. True freedom comes when you can rise above those difficulties, when you can live with joy in spite of the never-ending challenges.

To be without a care, is to be apart from life. To exist without obstacles, is to miss out on the fulfillment that comes from achieving in spite of the hurdles which must be overcome.

If your freedom depends on an escape from responsibility, you will always be running, and not be free at all. Don't deny your limitations. Don't hide from your problems. Make the effort necessary to transcend them. Something will always be holding you back. Go forward anyway, and you will be free.

Living the Wonder of It All

Blessings in the making

What would be the point of living if there were no challenges to overcome? What would give you joy if there was nothing that could bring you sadness? How could you feel warm if there was no such thing as cold? How could you know pleasure if there wasn't any pain?

Before you curse the darkness, consider that it provides the light with a place to shine. Before you curse the problems, keep in mind that they're what give value to the accomplishments.

Life's greatest treasures are those to which you give the most commitment. Challenges and difficult efforts are blessings in the making. The more you put into life, the more richly you will live it.

The dark days are filled with incredible opportunity. See that opportunity, know it and live it, and the bright days will be joyous indeed.

Something better

Consider for a moment all the valuable achievements which have come about because someone wasn't satisfied with the way things were. Throughout history, great leaps forward have been made by people who were seeking something better.

Time after time, something wasn't working as well as it could have, there were problems, shortcomings, issues that needed addressing, and someone addressed them. Someone saw what was wrong, envisioned something better, and then made it happen.

What we think of as progress is really a continuing positive response to dissatisfaction and frustration with the way things are. When things are not perfect, there is always a way to make them better.

Any time you experience frustration or dissatisfaction, see it as a clear signal to take a positive step toward something better. Your frustration is telling you there's a better way, and challenging you to make it real.

Life is filled with frustrations and because of them, it can continue getting better. When you feel strongly that there has to be a better way, there is. And you have the opportunity to find it.

Challenge or defeat?

When you're willing to accept challenge you won't have to accept defeat. Instead of throwing up your hands in defeat when things go wrong, look at the situation from a different perspective. See it as a challenge to be overcome.

Your attitude makes all the difference. Winners and losers are distinguished not by the circumstances they face, but by the way they face them. Losers think "I've been defeated." Winners think "I've been challenged."

Challenges are painful, inconvenient, and uncomfortable. They demand your time, your effort and your energy. And they make you stronger as a result.

Rather than accept defeat, see the challenge. Put the best that you have into getting past that challenge. It's easy to be a victim, but that won't get you anywhere. Be a victor instead, by accepting and transcending each challenge that comes your way.

Rare value

Diamonds have numerous practical applications in drills and other cutting tools, but that is not what makes diamonds so valuable. Authentic diamonds are valuable because they are so rare and difficult to come by.

That's useful to remember when you are faced with limitations. Those limitations give value to whatever you're working to accomplish. The more difficult the achievement, the more valuable it is.

Diamonds have value because you must dig long and hard in order to find one. If they were scattered around everywhere on the ground, they would not be worth much. In fact, you would probably have to pay someone if you wanted them hauled away.

So too with achievement. The things that come easy, with little or no effort, have little or no value. To create something of great value, you generally must overcome a challenge of great magnitude.

Are you digging for diamonds, or just shoveling dirt? Seek out the challenges. They are what bring value.

Opportunity

Opportunity is not a free ride. It is a challenge. And therein lies its value. Success cannot be handed to you. Accomplishment cannot be given to you. It's not something you happen upon. Being in the right place at the right time is worthless unless you make the effort to act on that opportunity.

Others can lead you to an opportunity or point one out to

you, but no one can give you opportunity. It is yours only when you begin to act upon it.

Opportunity is a compelling challenge to achieve. Challenge is one of the very best things you can ever experience. When you face challenge you learn, you grow, you reach, you discover truths, you discover yourself.

Challenge will bring out the best in you, and make it better. Do you sense an opportunity? Then take up the challenge. Success is yours if you make it, and no one is better than you at making the special success that you desire most fervently.

The muscles of success

If I went to a gym and attempted to bench press 250 pounds, I could not do it. Yet there are many people who can, because they have, through weight training, developed the necessary muscle strength to lift that much weight. The only way to develop the muscle strength for lifting heavy weights, is to start lifting lighter weights, and steadily work up to the desired weight.

The same concept applies to any kind of worthwhile accomplishment. You cannot expect to achieve a big success without first building your own muscles of success. Repeatedly lifting lighter weights will give you the strength to lift heavier weights. Similarly, every challenge you overcome gives you the strength to take on bigger challenges.

How strong are your muscles of success? Do you train and develop them every day by your willingness to take on tasks that truly challenge you? The strength needed for success in any endeavor is developed by repeatedly and effectively overcoming obstacles. Take on the challenges, and see how much stronger they make you.

Living the Wonder of It All

Make it big

To have what you want, to be the person you want to be, to do what you want with your life, make it important to you.

If all the daily details of life are preventing you from reaching your goal, then your goal is not big enough. To reach your goal, make it important. Make it big.

Visualize it in your mind, not in some little corner that gets attention once or twice a week, but front and center. Mentally put your goal in the way, blocking everything else.

Whatever you must look around, in order to see something else, will happen. Whatever you cannot avoid thinking of, will get accomplished. Instead of letting life get in the way of your goal, put your goal right smack in the way of your life. Do you really want it? That's the way to have it. Make it big in your mind, and you'll get there.

Living With
Purpose and Meaning

What is important to you?

If someone asked you to name the most important things in your life, what would you list — your family, your faith, your health, your integrity, your career? It is a question that very rarely gets asked of us by other people.

Yet, every day life asks that question. And every day we answer. The answer is not in words, but in actions. The actions you take on a daily basis speak louder than any claims you might make as to the most important things in your life. The way you spend your time, the things to which you give your attention, and the areas to which you commit your resources, present a clear and undeniable picture of your true priorities.

Are your priorities what you think they are? Look at your actions. Look at your results. Look at the life you've built for yourself. Does your reality agree with your vision? Success and fulfillment come not from what we think would be nice, but from what we actually do, hour after hour, day after day.

Your life at this moment is an accurate representation of the things that have truly been important to you in the past, a perfect picture of whatever you have been committed to achieving. With that in mind, ask yourself — what's important to you now?

What you cannot lose

When there are risks and challenges in every direction, where do you get the courage to move forward? That courage depends largely on the things you value most in your life.

When you place the most value on fleeting, shallow superficial things, you're constantly at risk of losing it all. Those things can quickly disappear. Money and material possessions are indeed very useful, and can bring a certain richness to life. Yet if you allow the value of your life to be defined by them, you're building on shaky ground.

On the other hand, if you value most those things you cannot lose, you'll have the courage necessary to assume the risks and to take on the difficult challenges. Your faith, your sincere love for others, your integrity, your purpose, your desire to make a difference, all have the power to survive whatever difficulties you may face.

Whatever happens, there are some things that can never be taken from you, some things you cannot lose. When those things matter most to you, it can give you the confidence to attempt just about anything.

The most important priorities

If everything in your entire life were suddenly taken away from you, what would you long for the most? What would you be unable to live without? No one likes to think about losing it all, but it can be a useful way to connect with your most important priorities.

What if you started every day by re-focusing yourself on the things which are truly important to you? How would that affect the way you go about each day? Certainly it would make you more focused, more disciplined, more effective, and more resilient to the slings and arrows of everyday life. Staying in touch with your true priorities provides a powerful and enabling perspective to every aspect of your life.

The more consistently you can maintain that perspective, the more fulfilling will be the results of your thoughts and actions. Every moment you're burning energy, making things happen. When you can keep all those things happening in accordance with the truly important aspects of your life, that life is indeed good.

Look past the superficial noise and clamor of the world around you. Discover what you truly value. Keep in touch with it on a moment by moment basis, and that which you value will add immense value to your world.

Ability and commitment

Greatness most often results not from extraordinary ability, but rather from ordinary ability followed through with extraordinary devotion. Commitment, depth of passion and clarity of purpose will elevate even the most ordinary, mundane efforts into the realm of truly great achievement.

Exceptional ability is a wonderful gift, though by itself it won't get you very far. More important than ability are desire and commitment. Without them, ability is useless. With them, any shortage of ability can be overcome.

Everyone alive has plenty of passion, though too often the true identity of that passion lies hidden. When you make the effort to understand and solidly connect with your passion, the result is an unyielding level of commitment to fulfilling that passion.

Whatever your level of ability, it will take you wherever you desire to go when energized with passion and commitment.

Why

It is helpful to know how to, yet that is not enough. It is also essential that you know why to. The "how to" of any achievement is usually fairly simple — rarely easy, but almost always simple. In most fields of endeavor, the path to success is fairly obvious, and is filled with plenty of effort and commitment.

So why do too few people follow that path? It's not the lack of knowing how. It is the failure to understand why.

With anything you reach for, if you are to have a chance of obtaining it, you must fashion a strong, solid and compelling connection to it. Unless your goals are personally meaningful, they are not likely to be achieved, no matter how clearly you understand what needs to be done to reach them.

Conversely, when you strive for something that is among your heart's deepest desires, even if you're not initially clear as to how you'll reach it, your strong sense of "why" will compel you to find a way.

Do you have trouble taking the actions you know you need to take in order to be successful? Maybe its because you're giving lip service to goals which don't truly match your innermost desires. Within you, there are purposes which will compel you to follow them. Seek them out and begin to live your incredible destiny.

Someone had a dream

The car you drive was designed and built because someone had a dream. The highway on which you travel is there because someone had a dream. The telephone you talk on and the worldwide network to which it is connected, was constructed because someone had a dream. Achievement begins with a dream.

Yet there are many, many dreams which wither and die without ever coming to pass. We will never know the benefits which they could have brought. Great accomplishments come about not only because someone dreamed of them, but also because someone believed in the dream enough to walk the long, hard road of making that dream a reality.

It takes a dream. And then it takes more than a dream. What is yours? And what are you doing about it? Stop and think for a moment about all the great things that have ever been achieved. Someone had a dream. Someone just like you. The world is filled with possibilities today. Take your pick, and then make it happen.

Frustration

Do you ever get frustrated? Have you ever been disappointed? Consider this. Frustration and disappointment come not from the circumstances. After all, the same situation can make one person totally frustrated while another person may not even give it a second thought.

Frustration and disappointment come from your own knowledge that things can be better. The only reason frustration is possible is your ability to visualize a better world. When you're frustrated it is because you have a positive vision, because you see and you know how much better life can be.

Think about it. Isn't that great? The next time you feel frustrated, remember that you're not simply frustrated or disappointed. Rather, you're busy envisioning a better world. Keep that in mind, and the frustration will become a positive force, focusing your mind not on the situation, but on the possibilities. Wrap yourself around the positive kernel of your frustration, and grow from there into something magnificent.

Use the energy of your frustration to follow the powerful possibilities which that frustration presumes.

Buried treasure

If you knew where an enormous treasure chest full of gold was buried, would you make the effort to dig it up? What if it took you two or three years to get to it? Would you still make the effort?

Chances are, you would keep digging for several years only if you were certain exactly where it was buried, and if you knew how much gold was there. If you weren't quite sure where it was, or what was in it, or whether it even existed, you might dig for a few days or weeks, and then move on to something else.

And therein lies the value of following a well defined plan to achieve clear, specific goals. When you know exactly what you're working toward, and you are confident that your efforts will get you there, then you'll do whatever it takes, for as long as it takes, to reach the goal. But if you're unsure of exactly what you're trying to accomplish, and you don't even know if you're making progress, it is all too easy to give up.

So be clear about what you want, and be precise in determining how to get it. The confidence you have about reaching your goal will provide the perseverance necessary to do it.

Possessions

Do you own your possessions, or do they own you? Your possessions include more than just the financial and material things to which you have title. You also possess such things as pride, knowledge, habits, assumptions, and opinions. All these possessions, material and otherwise, can be useful servants, but they are poor masters.

Consider pride, for example. Taking pride in your work, your appearance, and your performance compels you to do your best. Yet when pride is the driving reason behind what you do, it changes from a positive to a negative influence. Money can be the same way. In the service of a higher purpose, it is extremely useful, but when money becomes the ultimate objective it can be very destructive.

You have a wealth of possessions. They include everything from the change in your pocket to the opinions in your head. If you let them control you, they can become a disastrous burden. So keep them in perspective. They are your tools, not your purpose.

Commitment

How can you tell if you're fully committed to reaching a particular goal? It's easy. Commitment makes itself evident when the obstacles start to appear.

It's one thing to be excited about beginning a new pursuit. It is something altogether different to keep going long after the

Living the Wonder of It All

initial thrill has faded, when very real and very difficult challenges begin to emerge. Anyone can express their commitment in words. True commitment is shown by actions, by persistence, by the willingness to do whatever it takes.

The only way to be truly and irrevocably committed to a goal, is to make sure that the goal has meaning for you. You absolutely must find a way to personally relate to and connect with the goal. Make that connection, understand precisely what's in it for you, and your commitment will make it happen.

What are you trying to prove?

Do you spend your time and effort in a futile attempt to live up to someone else's standards? What are you trying to prove? And why? Fulfillment comes not from impressing others, but from being, as completely and magnificently as you can, the person you are.

Consider how much of your anxiety, worry and frustration come from your striving to live up to the expectations of others — to say the "right" things, drive the "right" kind of car, wear the "right" clothes. Of course we must be respectful and accepting of the people around us. We must also be careful not to become enslaved by their arbitrary definition of what has value and what doesn't.

Break free from the need to be accepted. The value of your life comes not from what others think of you. It comes from the degree to which you become the person you've always known you were meant to be. The admiration of others cannot be truly gained by chasing it. Paradoxically, the more you become your own person, the more you'll be admired by others.

Set your own standards, and set them high. Pursue excellence with sincerity. Forget about trying to prove anything. Just go ahead and be the best you can be.

Live what you are

When you know that what you're doing is right, what can possibly stop you? Believe in what you're doing, and you transcend doubt. Excuses become just a quaint and amusing memory when you have an unshakable belief in the value of your efforts.

The things you previously categorized as "good" or "bad" all take on a new definition — opportunity. Everything serves to move you forward, when your commitments and efforts are in step with your convictions.

The way to truly believe in what you do, is to do what you truly believe in. It is a waste of time and energy to try and adjust your beliefs to fit your circumstances. How can you accomplish anything when you're working against yourself? Effectiveness, success and fulfillment come when you adjust your circumstances to fit your beliefs. That is most certainly a challenge, and one that is well worth the effort.

Dream big dreams

If the obstacles get larger and more daunting, respond by reaching higher. Make your dreams bigger than your difficulties. The things that hold you back are limited and finite, yet the dreams which push you forward have no limits. No matter how formidable the problem, you can always find a desire that is even stronger.

Take a day off. Get away from your routine. Go somewhere

Living the Wonder of It All

you've never gone. Get some distance and some perspective, and then consider this. The world is brimming with opportunity, and there's no reason for you to be left behind. Now is the perfect time to build the life you want, to become whatever you want, to create, to go places, to make a difference.

Dream big dreams, and make full use of their energizing effect. You can have any life you want, so make it the best you can imagine.

The power of passion

If you do not like your present circumstances, stop giving your thoughts and your energy to them. Rather than being sick and tired of the way things are, become passionate about how you want them to be.

You can attract to yourself whatever you most passionately desire. Yet you can also attract whatever you most passionately despise. Whatever is the object of your strongest, most enduring passion will become a reality in your life. So focus your passion on what you love, not on what you hate.

Imagine what would happen if you spent this entire day with all your energy directed toward your most positive possibilities. Imagine how life would be if you could simply accept that what's happened has happened, and now you're free to fulfill your most treasured desires.

Imagine it, and then go beyond imagining to make it so. Set your mind, your heart, your intention and your passion on the very best, and that is where you'll go.

Your Precious Life

Life is precious. Even from a highly cynical viewpoint one cannot escape the conclusion that life is in fact miraculous. The most objective, empirical evidence shows physical life, and the universe which surrounds it, to be a wondrous creation, something which, if it did not exist, would be far beyond all but the most ambitious of imaginations. And then there is life's spiritual component, not as easily defined or objectively observed, yet a significant and fundamental part of human life nonetheless.

In our day-to-day existence, we tend to forget about the fact that we're alive and part of an incredibly awesome universe. We mostly take it for granted. We stand in line to buy lottery tickets when in fact we have each already won the most stunningly generous lottery that could ever be imagined.

You may well fantasize about what you would do if you won ten million dollars. But what are you doing with the life you already have, which is worth far, far more than ten million dollars? You are alive in spite of unimaginable odds. Whatever limitations you may see in your life, your blessings and treasures far outweigh them.

You've always known this. Yet how often do you really think about it? How often do you take it into consideration when making decisions or setting priorities? You seek to have success, and you cannot get it because you already have it. Your objective is not to become successful, but rather to honor and fully utilize the ultimate success that is already yours, the success of being you. In other words, life is not about getting more, but rather about being more.

Indeed, what would you do with that ten million dollars, or ten billion? And why are you not already doing it? You have a mission. Your rare and precious life has a purpose. Fulfillment will never come from finding excuses to avoid that purpose. Fulfillment comes from uncovering, understanding and following that purpose.

No consultant, guru or mystical incantations can tell you that purpose. You already know it on some level. It is evidenced by your likes and dislikes, your interests, your achievements, your frustrations, your pleasures and your pains. It becomes a little more clear each day, especially if that day is spent in earnest thought and diligent effort.

You live at a time in which possibilities are expanding faster than you can even comprehend them. Many of the possibilities are good; many are not so good. Others are tragic. And then there are some which are truly magnificent.

The great thing is that you always have a choice. The whole world has a choice. Making the best choices depends on understanding their value. That calls for clearly seeing them in context. And the context is this grand and glorious existence we know as life.

Too often we limit our possibilities by confining their context. Too often we forget how far we have already come, and thus fail to see how far we can possibly go. We endure enormous strife in order to get a few pieces of silver, when we're already standing atop a mountain of gold. We focus so intently on our problems and limitations. Yet we overlook the fact that those problems and limitations are discernible only because of our very capacity to transcend them.

Every day you face plenty of challenges, obstacles which are very real and very difficult. Yet it would be impossible to even know about these challenges, much less experience them as such, if you were down on their level. The fact is, you are far superior to any challenge you'll ever face. You are more ro-bust, by orders of magnitude, than any obstacle that will ever confront you. You are the miraculous, living you, alive and effective.

So what do you do with all this? How do you live up to the possibilities which permeate your very being? That is a ques-tion which has an infinite number of answers. But for you, right now at this moment, there is a very specific and compel-ling answer. In some way, on some level, you know what that answer is. Look past the troubles of this day. Look past the trivial concerns. Look past your immediate frustrations, an-noyances, obsessions and distractions, past the pains, the plea-sures and the discomforts. Reach inside and ask yourself why you care about these things anyway. Connect to that underly-ing why, to the part of you that is fundamentally essential to the real, living person you are.

You are wise to be concerned about you bank account, your voice mail messages, the oil in your car, the food in your pan-try. These are things which, if managed with care and atten-tion, can help you to fulfill your purpose and destiny. Yet when you become so consumed with the external, material things that you lose sight of who you are, you become a slave to your own trivialities rather than a master of your own fortune.

Always remember that there is a purpose to your life. The

reason you take care of the daily details is so that you may better serve that purpose. But the details are not the purpose. If life seems too empty, it means you're focused on the wrong things. Life by its very definition is overflowing with richness. It cannot be empty, but your pursuits at any given time might very well be.

To bring fullness and abundance to your own life, live like you are someone special, because you truly are. Certainly there are bills to be paid, appointments to be kept, and other details that beg for your attention. Keep in mind, however, that you're doing these things for a reason. In the service of that purpose, you have chosen to attend to all the details. You are in control of all these things. They are not in control of you.

The degree to which you value, celebrate and utilize the good fortune of your life will determine the fullness and richness of that life. You already have more than you could ever possibly use. Your challenge is to make the most of it on a moment by moment basis. Let's consider some of the many aspects of your life, and how you can give value to them.

You are blessed with a powerful, intelligent mind. Fill it with knowledge. Challenge it to grow and to become more powerful by constantly putting it to work. You can think and you can reason, and those skills have the power to take you anywhere you wish to go. Consider for a moment what life would be like if you could not think. Then consider what life would be like if you could expand your thinking by just a little bit each day. Your mind is indeed a powerful creation, and it is in your best interest to use that mind to the fullest extent possible.

The thoughts you think do not happen by accident. There's a reason for them. Pay attention to what you're thinking. Give your mind the credit it's due. Follow through on those thoughts. Keep them alive, nurture them and give them the energy of your effort. You've got a great mind. Make full use of the treasures it offers you.

You have a magnificent and useful body which permits you to move from place to place, to sense the world around you in its richness and detail, to manipulate objects in countless ways, to build, to create, and to express yourself. That body may not be perfect, but it is your home and it serves you well. Take good care of it. Nourish your body with top quality nutrition. Keep it strong and healthy with regular physical exercise. Constantly cleanse and sustain it by drinking clean water and breathing clean air.

Your desires are pointers to your purpose. Not only do they motivate you to achieve great things, they also can reveal your true essence. Pay attention to your desires. Seek to understand them. They represent a powerful path toward self awareness. Too often, desires get corrupted as they make their way into your consciousness. For example, the desire for more nutritious food can often get interpreted as simply a desire for more junk food. That's why it is important to look for the desires behind the desires. Often, understanding a desire can be more useful than simply following it. Every desire has a reason. Behind that reason is another reason. Dig deeply enough into your desires and you'll gain a valuable understanding about the driving force behind your life. Experience your desires, seek to understand them and they will enrich your life.

The things which you are interested in and passionate about can take you a long way. Whatever you enjoy doing, is a gift you've been given. It is your own unique contribution to the world. It will take you anywhere you want to go if you will take the time and effort to develop it. When you cultivate your own unique talents, you gain confidence, and a larger vision of yourself. That will have a positive influence on every part of your life. Value your interests and passions, and work to develop them. Put forth a sustained, consistent effort in this direction. Do something every day to develop your skills and knowledge in the things which interest you. Know that there's a powerful reason for whatever you enjoy doing. Your enjoyment is life's way of motivating you to excel in an area where you have a skill and a desire to make a difference. Put that motivation to work for you.

Your disappointments are also a valuable part of your life. Like your desires, they point you toward your purpose. Whenever you experience disappointment, it's because something did not work out the way you intended. Of course you can learn from that in a practical sense. Your disappointments will help you to discover what doesn't work, and thereby bring you closer to understanding what does work. Yet beyond that, your disappointments reveal the things about which you care the most. Out of disappointment, comes a deeper sense of appreciation and a clearer understanding of what's important to you. Disappointment can be painful. That's why it is so powerful. Value and make the best of your disappointments by first admitting them, then experiencing them, and then understanding the very positive and life affirming aspects within you which make those disappointments possible.

Experience joy. Drink in and value the joyful times in your life. Experience them fully. A moment of true, unencumbered joy is worth more than pure gold. You'll think more clearly, be more motivated, feel better and be healthier, when you regularly lose yourself in joy. Relish the experience of being fully alive and letting yourself completely enjoy yourself. Is such behavior selfish? No. When you have more joy in your own life, you have more to give others. By experiencing joy, you enable the true person inside to come to life. That person is overflowing with love, abundance and creativity which will add immensely to your life and the lives of those around you. Let yourself be joyful, without guilt, without expectations. Truly value the joyful moments and lose yourself in their richness. You'll feel the power of that joy in every part of your life.

The other people in this world with whom you come in contact represent an extremely valuable aspect of your life. Your relationships with others can add immensely to the richness of your life. The more you value, appreciate, understand and serve those around you, the more fulfillment your own life will have. By yourself, you are quite powerful and capable. And when you join your efforts with others, the list of possibilities expands exponentially. The value you direct toward others is reflected back to you many times over.

The challenges you face can bring great value to your life. Challenge compels you to grow, to build, to create, to excel. Challenge can motivate. It can quickly teach you new skills and help you make new contacts. It builds confidence and competence. Remember that the challenges are not there to stop you. The challenges are there to help you grow, to help you be the person who can attain the dream you're following. In fact, the person you become in the pursuit of your dream is worth far more than the fulfillment of that dream could ever be. Challenge can energize your life like nothing else. What you gain from facing challenges can never be taken away from you. Value and appreciate challenge by having the courage to seek it out. Make challenge a part of your experience every day. A big enough challenge will force you to be the best you can be. It will bring out strengths and abilities you never knew you had. It will teach you about yourself, and make you truly alive with possibilities.

Value the beauty in your life. Your own beauty comes not from

Living the Wonder of It All

the color of your hair or the clothes you wear, but from your ability to appreciate, value and identify with the abundance of beauty which exists in the world around you. No one can really say what beauty is, but everyone knows it when they see it. Beauty has its physical manifestations, but it goes far beyond the material world. Beauty talks in the language of the heart. The magnificence of a sunset, or of a violin concerto, cannot be adequately conveyed in words. Just as food nourishes your body, beauty nourishes your spirit. It can inspire and challenge you to do great things.

These are just some of the many valuable aspects of your life, the things which make you unique and precious. They are things which truly matter and which will make an enormous difference in the quality and fulfillment of your life.

You are special. You are rare and precious. You know that. There is no one else just like you. You have a unique contribution to make, a extraordinary expression of life to offer the rich universe around you. The extent to which you fully express your true essence, is the extent to which your own special destiny will be fulfilled. You have possibilities which no one else has ever even dreamt of. Make them real and make the most of your precious and wondrous life.

Web Links

The following Internet web links are provided to expand and enhance the material in this book. These websites are free and available to anyone who wishes to visit, with no cost or registration required. Please enjoy them and feel free to recommend them to others.

The Daily Motivator - a new positive message every Monday through Saturday, plus an archive of more than 2,500 previous messages.

www.DailyMotivator.com

The Wonder of It All - a picture and music presentation of the poem on pages 8-9 of this book.

www.WonderOfItAll.com

Right Now - the original, enormously popular picture and music presentation from The Daily Motivator that has been enjoyed by millions of people around the world. The text of the Right Now presentation appears on pages 157-158 of this book.

www.PositivePause.com

Even Now - a calming, insightful picture and music presentation for a troubled world.

www.PositivePause.com/en

Peace Beyond Words - sample clips from the CD of original music composed and performed by Paul Baker for The Daily Motivator.

www.PeaceBeyondWords.com